Emma Norman

Howard Norman is the author of five novels, including *The Haunting of L.*, *The Bird Artist*, and *Northern Lights*. He lives with his family in Vermont and Washington, D.C.

ALSO BY HOWARD NORMAN

The Northern Lights

The Chauffeur

The Bird Artist

The Museum Guard

The Haunting of L.

My Famous Evening

IN FOND REMEMBRANCE OF ME

IN FOND
REMEMBRANCE
OF ME

Howard Norman

PICADOR

Farrar, Straus and Giroux

New York

www.picadorusa.com

Picador® is a U.S. registered trademark and is used by Farrar, Straus and Giroux
under license from Pan Books Limited.

For information on Picador Reading Group Guides, as well as ordering, please
contact Picador.
Phone: 646-307-5629
Fax: 212-253-9627
E-mail: readinggroupguides@picadorusa.com

Some portions of this book appeared in *TriQuarterly* and the *Princeton University
Library Chronicle*, vol. LXIII.

Designed by Jonathan D. Lippincott

Library of Congress Cataloging-in-Publication Data
Norman, Howard A.
    In fond remembrance of me / Howard Norman.
        p.   cm.
    ISBN 0-312-42522-8
    EAN 978-0-312-42522-7
    1. Tanizaki, Helen, d. 1978.   2. Folklorists—Canada—Biography.
3. Folklorists—Japan—Biography.   4. Inuit—Folklore.   5. Tales—
Manitoba—Churchill.   6. Inuit literature—Canada—Translations into
English.   I. Title.

GR55.T26N67 2005
398'.092—dc22
[B]
                                                          2004056097

First published in the United States by Farrar, Straus and Giroux

First Picador Edition: February 2006

10   9   8   7   6   5   4   3   2   1

for Jonathan Galassi

What good is intelligence if you cannot discover a useful melancholy?

—Ryunosuke Akutagawa

IN FOND

REMEMBRANCE

OF ME

———————

INTRODUCTION

On November 8, 1977, in the Halifax train station a few minutes before boarding a train for Montreal, Helen Tanizaki handed me a letter from the afterlife. At least that is the impression she intended by its title, *In Fond Remembrance of Me*, written on the envelope. "Do not open until—" she had said. Helen had no need to complete the sentence; I knew how it ended. She had been diagnosed with fatal stomach cancer and was going home to spend her final months with her brother and sister-in-law in Kyoto, Japan.

This book is about my friend Helen Tanizaki, linguist, translator, diarist, prodigious writer of letters, who had lived and worked throughout the Canadian arctic as well as Greenland and Siberia. Mainly she translated oral literature—myths, poems, songs—and life histories in these places. I knew Helen in Churchill, Manitoba, in 1977 during September and October, the first week of November in Halifax, and in letters sent from Japan until her death in the summer of 1978. We had not known of each other's existence before meeting at the end of August 1977 at the Beluga Motel set along the Churchill River (George and John Hicks, Prop.). She stayed in Room 10, I was in Room 1, "bookends," as Helen put it. I had arrived armed only with a rudimentary training in ethnographic linguistics, some knowledge of the structure of the folktale gained in graduate studies at the Folklore Institute at Indiana University, and having had a very basic tutorial in the Inuit dialect spoken along the western coast of Hudson Bay. Quite soon I not only met Helen but learned that in a sense we were in Churchill for the same reason. We had both been employed—me by a museum, she by a publisher—to translate narratives told by a man named Mark Nuqac, an Inuit elder. I would of course be translating the stories into English, Helen would translate them into Japanese. It was quite the unforeseen synchronicity of lives, let alone linguistic endeavor; Mark Nuqac absolutely adored Helen and could scarcely tolerate my presence, and there is not a splinter of exaggeration in saying as much.

And it worked out rather well. In this regard, my time in Churchill certainly "tested my mettle." Equally unforeseen were the rewards I found in Helen's difficult friendship, which I trust will be clear throughout these pages. I was twenty-eight, born in Toledo, Ohio, with a makeshift education and not very self-reflective, to put it bluntly; Helen, perhaps the most introspective person I've known, was thirty-nine, born in London and raised in Japan, a Ph.D. in linguistics. In most respects we were from opposite ends of the earth.

A few years ago while organizing an archive of manuscripts, travel diaries, photographs, letters, etc., to be deposited in Special Collections at Boston University, I rediscovered the loose-leaf notebook journals I kept during my stay in Churchill. I was surprised and pleased to find out how dedicated I was to these journals, though I remember writing in them late at night, because in Churchill I hardly slept. That period of insomnia was due in large part to a general undercurrent of anxiety, much work at hand, a caffeine habit, and I suppose a general sense of agitation and befuddlement at how peculiar and frictional my working relationship with Mr. Nuqac was from the get-go. Anyway, the journals served as the basis for *In Fond Remembrance of Me.*

Of course, I was not a stenographer of Helen's and my conversations; however, I was quite diligent in transcribing and chronicling each day's and evening's events, social incidents, conversations (largely with Helen and Mr. Nuqac), my own vexations and musings and occasional disquisitions on the translation process itself. In reading and rereading these journals, I felt it all again with vivid immediacy, let alone perhaps the most intense nostalgia I have ever experienced. Nostalgia for a formative period can become an intensifying element in one's life—it did for me, at least, as it pertains to the writing of this book. I knew during that autumn something interesting was happening in my life, but on reflection I can scarcely claim that at the time I had even a modest comprehension of just how much intellectual—and, yes, spiritual—life Helen had introduced me to. I admit that I became quite fixed in Helen's orbit—that is, I began to calibrate my ignorance in (and newfound intoxication with) certain philosophical, spiritual, and literary subjects against Helen's strong opinions and far deeper levels of engagement. That is partly what I mean by *formative*; I was getting educated. As for the metaphysics of being in someone's orbit, I must add that, emotionally, we managed to remain at a fixed distance from each other. (At the time I did not think I was in *love* with Helen; looking back, I think that I was at least enamored of her.) This is more specifically to say that we did not have an erotic relationship, unless the one dream I gratefully had of kissing Helen is taken into account. (I dutifully entered it in my journal.) No dream is perhaps innocent. In that dream, however, we were neither standing upright nor lying down, but slanted, entwined together at a 45-degree angle, and what's more were levitated a few feet aboveground, an impossible feat, of course, except if sponsored by a dream-based physics—or, for that matter, depicted in an Inuit drawing from, say, Eskimo Point along Hudson Bay, in which a dog, arctic fox, seal, polar bear, or human being may be likewise positioned in time and space as Helen and I were in my dream. When I reported this dream to Helen, her reply was, "Sounds exhausting."

This book contains eleven narratives told by Mark Nuqac. I heard twenty-three, but only eleven of my translations survived Mark's, Helen's, and a few other Inuit elders' tough scrutiny and argument in order to reside in these pages. Believe me, I am grateful for that many. Mr. Nuqac called them "my Noah stories." I write extensively about what it was like to hear these stories and attempt to transcribe and translate them in Mark's presence, incorporating Helen's criticism, editing, and linguistic know-how. As for their common plots, I also delve into that throughout this memoir, or recollection, or collage of memories. Suffice it to say that each story recounts what, in Mr. Nuqac's thinking, was a historical incident of great import: Noah's Ark has drifted into the arctic waters of Hudson Bay—this enormous wooden ship with its cargo of all manner of strange beast (many delectable, at least by the look of them)—and has drawn, to say the least, the curiosity of Inuit villagers living along the coast. As each story unfolds, the presence of the ark along with Noah's intractable nature engenders an array of incidents (some fatal), dramatic and comic and otherwise, all highly memorable, some—as Helen put it—"as zany as I've ever heard in the arctic." It is a collision of cultures—as if life were not unpredictable enough!

I have since read and heard different Inuit "flood myths," which refer to the received story of Noah's Ark; that is, God gets angry at the prodigiously untoward behavior of human beings, drowns everyone but Noah's family and two of each kind of animal, and sails the ark off into wandering exile for forty days and forty nights. (Mark Nuqac once derided this punishment, as much as calling it mild; and no wonder, considering that in the stories he must've been raised on, when terrible social violations took place, a person might be exiled for life to the most severely barren of locales, killed, or possibly have to live inside a polar bear's anus.) In Mr. Nuqac's stories the Old Testament figure of Noah is complicated. Stranger in a strange land, eventually—often abruptly—he falls victim to his own haplessness and bewilderment at best, blind stubbornness at worst—all the while placing his family and animal passengers in great jeopardy. He becomes overwhelmed by winter. Throughout the Noah stories there are many anecdotes of Noah's becoming quite unhinged. "Well, wouldn't *you*," Helen once said, "fall apart, if your ship got locked in ice, you got very claustrophobic, the cries of seagulls were driving you nuts—not to mention, every so often, you saw a giraffe or hippopotamus wander out across the ice and disappear. I imagine I'd become unhinged, too!"

Mr. Nuqac was remarkable; Helen was remarkable; and I had the good fortune of spending time with both. For many reasons—lack of knowing how to live in the present moment, too much emotional and other data coming in too swiftly, a kind of stuttering quality to my intellect, the basic conundrum of inexperience, or all of these in concert—I did not rise to the occasion of being in Helen's and Mark's compelling company. I assert this as a simple fact of life. I feel some shame in it and much regret, insofar as shame and regret are so often the twin bequeathings of memory. I only wish I might've been more poised.

How best to organize and, to some extent, reorder experience? This book has thematic and structural asymmetries; it is comprised, if you will, of overlapping panels of reality; certain words and phrases which came to have for me something of an iconic presence ricochet between chapters, in an enlivening way I hope. And of course Inuit folktales are woven throughout. On occasion—not often, but still—I collated together several conversations Helen and I had on the same subject (birds, mostly), and I purposely mitigated or left out certain exchanges (mostly about her illness) as a way of being vigilant toward sentimentality. Naturally, I wanted a sense of dailiness to preside. ("If only the rain and the flying cranes would enter themselves into my diary," wrote Helen's most beloved writer, Ryunosuke Akutagawa.) The most dignified literary ambition here is to verisimilitude. To this end, the book's structure is symphonic in that certain emotional—even obsessive—refrains are featured, whereas certain subjects are at intervals soloists: that of *melancholy*, *birds*, *language*, *Japanese writers*, *the typewriter as existential relic*, *the afterlife*—all of which were Helen's inspired and inspiring preoccupations.

When I was growing up there were no books in my various houses, no books to speak of, except a set of encyclopedias, though I first encountered the arctic—saw my first photographs of Inuit people, polar bears, almost incomprehensible vast reaches of snow and ice—in *Life* and *The Saturday Evening Post* and *Look*, magazines that occasionally had features on so-called exotic and certainly far-flung places and cultures, as well as books found on the shelves of the bookmobile I worked in at age fourteen. Eleven years later I found myself in the actual arctic; three years after that I met Helen Tanizaki in Churchill.

I do recall that my family subscribed to *Reader's Digest*. Each issue contained a generic piece called "My Most Unforgettable Character." The idea was to profile and generally extol the virtues of a person who by sheer force of personality or by fate or happenstance exerted indispensable influence on and deeply enriched the writer's life. I don't in the least hesitate to call Helen far and away my most unforgettable character. She had quite a life, Helen did; she was an ardent spirit inside a lucid intelligence, a woman who drew great clarity and affirmation from personal tragedy and who toward the end of her life reinvented herself as "a bird of the sea and cliffs," that is, subscribed to her very own idea of reincarnation. I am thoroughly convinced from her final letters that Helen completely trusted that possibility. And who's

to say?—perhaps she did become a seabird. My most unforgettable character. Memory is more a séance than anything,
replete with the desire to resurrect original presences and attendant emotions. After boarding the train for Montreal,
Helen said, "Don't forget me." And I have tried not to.

Part I

WOMAN TYPING ARCTIC

WOMAN TYPING ARCTIC

One evening when I stepped into her room in the Beluga Motel, where, from the dock, beluga whales could be sighted feeding in the Churchill River, Helen looked up from her typewriter. "Just now I saw myself in the mirror and noticed that my illness has turned my face into the face of my old aunt's," she said in her slight British accent. "My old aunt hunched over her big sewing machine in Japan. Of course, it's my own face. And I'm obviously not bent over a sewing machine but my typewriter. Typing up the arctic, as usual, right? That's all I've really done with my life, if I'm honest about it . . . except for my brief marriage. Except for my brief marriage, all I've done is type up the arctic, and so have I had a useful life, then? You tell me. Go from place to place and type up my reports and my translations and write all those letters. Look at all the pages! Type, type, type."

"Feeling sorry for yourself, or just philosophical, or what?" I said.

"The philosophical ones naturally get the saddest, don't they? I see a particular faraway look on a child's face, on a back road out in *nowheresville*"—Helen loved picking up the odd American slang—"and I can tell what she's in for her whole life. Oh, sure, I recognize the look. Some days I wish

I hadn't thought so much, you know? But I've wished that since I was a little girl."

I looked around the sparsely furnished room, standard motel fare, I suppose. White walls. Helen had draped colorful Buddhist prayer flags over her bed; I had to ask what they were. There were stacks of Japanese novels bound in twine, placed on the floor and bedside table. The Underwood typewriter on the desk. Linguistics notebooks bound in twine. Diaries. Correspondences. Foreign postage stamps steamed off and glued in a ledger. Rubber-tipped glue dispenser. Steamer trunk with torn silk lining, secured by a buckle and length of leather belt. Notebook after notebook of ornithological jottings, birds seen when and where, the neat columns. Latin names in parentheses. Field guides in French, Japanese, English, Dutch. I think that I recall a German-language guide, too. She seemed to have set up this room as a kind of garret—except not in a Parisian attic under a sloping tiled roof, but in a motel surrounded by tundra and arctic sea—dedicated to thinking and writing.

It was already cold in August. "I seem to sleep better in cold climates," Helen said. "I can't say why, really."

Taped to Helen's typewriter was a quote in Japanese (which she translated for me) from Ryunosuke Akutagawa: *What good is intelligence if you cannot discover a useful melancholy?*

I then thought—right as I was looking at her—that Helen had a kind of unrequited love with the world. In a letter dated March 19, 1978, and sent from Kyoto, she wrote: "I've been blessed in getting to work with dignified peoples in remote and beautiful parts of the world. I got to 'dwell in beloved chill sunrises,' as Basho said. I have heard wonderful stories. I have seen birds far from where I was born. But I wasn't given enough time. I simply wasn't. I do not feel forgiving about that. I'm referring to Fate. This dying, it's an insult. I'm grateful for what I was given. But I feel insulted."

DON'T FORGET ME

Before Billy Umiaq stepped into the Hudson's Bay Company store to buy cigarettes, he turned to his friends and said, "Don't forget me."

How long might such a purchase take? Five, ten minutes? His friends waited outside. Roughly ages thirteen, fourteen, fifteen, they smoked cigarettes, struck various postures of self-doubt and self-adoration, agitated cool, as though alternating between conformity and sudden alienation that no doubt animates teenagers most anywhere on the planet. For these Inuit young people it was, I suspect, an average night in Churchill, Manitoba, whose chamber of commerce advertises it as "The Polar Bear Capital of the World." They had all been to a showing of *Phantom Lady*, a film noir starring Ella Raines, Alan Curtis, and Franchot Tone. Drenched in moodiness, rain-slicked streets, and shadowy atmosphere—a classic noir thriller—the story revolves around the attempts by a character named Carol Richman to clear her boss of a murder he did not commit. His alibi, a woman who was with him at the time of the murder and has since disappeared, falls apart when no one who saw them together will admit it. As she stalks suspects to save the man she loves, Carol faces danger at every turn. There is a bartender killed in a street brawl, a jazz drummer strangled as he is revealing information, an insane woman, and the psychopathic friend of her boss. In other words, just about as urban and therefore opposite a milieu as possible from Churchill, Manitoba.

Helen and I had front-row seats (two shipping crates) for the grainy print of *Phantom Lady*. It was shown on the cracked alabaster wall of the luggage room in the Churchill train station. There were about forty people in attendance. All the alienation and morally compromised obsession of the main characters seemed only to confirm suspicions of city life and put, as far as I could detect, the audience in good spirits. Throughout the movie, the old-fashioned crank-and-sprocket school projector had broken down only twice. That was luck. People sat on luggage of all shapes and sizes. Leaning against the back wall, Billy Umiaq and his pals were in constant banter, once in a while making a real show-off ruckus of catcalls and laughter. Everyone put up with everything. The movie ended and then it was time for a smoke.

"Don't forget me," Billy said. The stars were out but it was not dark; September, daylight lengthening out into the night hours, a kind of crepuscular light presiding. I was standing with Helen near the store. I wanted to get back to my own typewriter. When Billy emerged he was already tapping a cigarette from the pack onto the palm of his hand. "Hey, how you been?" he said to his friends.

The heartbreaking, indelible resonance of those two simple sentences, "Don't forget me," and, "Hey, how you been?" spoken scarce few minutes apart—words of departure and reunion; alas, Billy had come back from a journey safe and sound.

"Don't forget me" did not strike a cynical note but rather evoked the philosophy of precariousness. This is logical; life *is* precarious. That was useful knowledge. All one needed to do was to listen carefully to traditional Inuit stories to learn how suddenly life can change.

No single story can be said to epitomize this, but many share certain basic conundrums, narrative trajectories that move from order to chaos, from joyfulness to mourning. In such stories, for example, a man says good-bye to his wife and children. The day is sunny, the air crisp, life is fine and hopeful. A person can see far into the distance. "Good-bye, husband," he hears. "Good-bye, father." And this man sets out on his sled. The dogs are behaving well. The man has prayed for a successful day of hunting or fishing, the ability and luck to provide for his family.

Yet ill fate may well lie in ambush. In folktales the possibilities are endless. A ten-legged polar bear maligned or insulted long ago may choose to exact revenge on human beings—*this one*—not an hour's walk from the village. The ice may crack open and the hunter plummet after his dogs into a fissure. The arctic hosts a vast repertoire of spirits, some benevolent, others who would readily half-orphan the children of that hunter at whim. Most often the hunter makes it out and back and lives to tell the tale. Still, it is always a good idea to say, "Don't forget me."

Each journey, as Buddhists say, begins with the first step, such as Billy Umiaq's step into the Hudson's Bay Company store. It is not paranoia to say that life is unpredictable; unpredictability is part of quotidian life. You temper it with a shrug. "Hey, how you been?" You acknowledge it and move on. Neither the actual amount of time that has passed nor the distance traveled points to the central meaning. It was that Billy Umiaq had disappeared from view, and now he was back. Life had worked out for the best.

Helen could not afford to catch a cold or, worse, pneumonia; she had had pneumonia twice in eighteen months. We should have gone directly back to the motel. For some reason, however, I began a disquisition, replete with half-baked theories, about the movie's larger themes and implications. Being someone who had difficulty disguising her immediate responses to almost anything, Helen grimaced slightly. "Where did this come from?" she said. "What are you talking about?" Helen was of small physical stature and yet responses registered on her face in big ways—I equated it to the outsized expressions required by background characters in an opera, as if the audience is keenly observing only them. Her face could fall into solemn disappointment, it could squinch up in disgust, it could submit to a rubbery pout as if gravity itself were forcing a clownish frown. There was a huge full moon flooding the tundra. I just kept talking—". . . I mean, the way she just knew from the beginning her boss didn't kill anybody. Plus, there were no— what? *normal* people in that movie. I guess it's all about how sinister life is, huh?"—until Helen finally interrupted me. "Howard Norman," she said—she always used my full name—"you've taken a simple plot and . . ." She stopped, exasperated, scarcely able to catch her breath. We stood in silence a moment, breaths pluming ghostily into the night air. Perhaps from a distance we seemed to be squaring off. We heard a burst of laughter from near the store. "That's all,"

Helen said. "That's all. I guess I'm not up to discussing this now. I really enjoyed the movie, that's all."

In memory it is a still life, "The Argument," call it. Was it that, an argument? I think, yes, because our voices must have carried a certain pitch of annoyance. The Inuit teenagers kept looking over. Maybe they were expecting something more. They lit up cigarettes; they lit each other's cigarettes. Helen and I escorted each other to our separate rooms in the Beluga Motel.

Around 5 a.m. the next morning when I woke, I saw that a note had been slid under my door: *The movie was about a woman who did not give up on love. Life's gotten away from you—if you cannot see that!*

"Looking back on it"—this is from Helen's letter of March 27, 1978—"I consider our friendship lovely, hermetic, difficult." Helen had a way with words; besides which, I don't contest her opinion.

NOAH BECOMES A GHOST

There's different stories you hear about this fellow, Noah—in church and other places, you hear stories. Here's what I know happened. It happened a long time ago. One day, a big wooden boat floated into Hudson Bay. People from the village nearby paddled out to it in kayaks. Ice was just forming along the edges—it was almost winter.

They paddled out, and when they got to the boat, a man shouted, "Who's on this boat? Whose boat is this?"

"My name is Noah," a man shouted down. "My wife, son,

and daughter are with me. It's too cold here—we're going away."

This made the villagers laugh in their kayaks—"No, no, no— here comes winter!" With this, winter arrived and the big boat was surrounded by floating pieces of ice.

"What?—What?—What?" said Noah. "Get us out, get us out."

"Not until the ice-break-up," a village man said.

"Take us into your village," said Noah's wife.

"How can you say that—how can you say that?" Noah said.

With this, Noah's wife, daughter, and son jumped into kayaks and were paddled to the village. Paddled past pieces of ice—pieces of ice were all around, bumping against the kayaks. When Noah's wife, son, and daughter turned to look back, they saw that the ark was now stuck in the ice!

In the village, Noah's wife, son, and daughter were given a place to live. They were given food to eat. They were given warm clothes. One night, Noah's wife said to the villagers, "On our travels, we had a lot of big animals on the ark. But then we got hungry. Our other food ran out. It was raining hard. The rain didn't stop. We ate some animals. Then we arrived at this place. We didn't know how to get home. We got lost up here. That's what happened."

"Did any of the animals taste good?" a village woman asked.

"Some did—some didn't," Noah's wife said.

"Give us their names," a man said.

"Giraffe"—this made everyone fall to laughing. "Hippopotamus—" this made everyone fall to laughing.

But each day, Noah's wife was deep in worry and sadness. She stood at the edge of the ice to see if her husband was walking from the ark. Then one morning she called out, "Look—!" Everyone saw a polar bear walking across the ice. Following the bear was a fox. Following the fox was a raven—walking, hopping along, flying a little. Following the raven was Noah, crawling. "What is my husband doing?" Noah's wife cried out.

A village man said to Noah's wife, "A bear walks along—it kills a seal, it drags it up and eats some. The fox might run in fast and grab a scrap or two. Then—next—next—the raven can fly in fast and grab a scrap or two."

"Oh—oh—oh!" said Noah's wife. "So lastly my husband might get something to eat."

"At least he's found a way to get something to eat," the man said.

"If I pry off a plank of wood, will you leave my husband some food?" she said.

"Yes," the man said.

With this, Noah's wife walked out to the ark. She pried off a plank of wood and carried it back to the village. The villagers used it to start a fire. Everyone sat by it—and then some men went out on the ice and left scraps of seal meat and fish for Noah. First, the fox grabbed a little—it ran off. Then a raven got some—it flew off. But Noah got some food, too.

Then it happened that the bear went a long time without killing a seal. It got very hungry. One day, it turned and chased the fox, but the fox knew how to get away. The bear scattered off the raven—and then it caught this Noah, killed him, out on the ice. When news of this reached Noah's wife, she wept—her daughter wept, her son wept.

More planks were taken from the ark. One night, Noah's wife stood by the sea ice and saw the ghost of her husband walking in the southerly direction. "Where are you going?" she shouted out to him.

"Home," he said. "Get our son and daughter—all three can come with me."

"No," said Noah's wife, sadly, but she said it. "You leave—I will stay here with our daughter and son. That is how it must be. That is how it will be." Noah kept walking—a ghost going in the southerly direction over ice.

Noah's wife told everyone in the village what had happened. On her long travels, Noah's wife had seen many things. Her husband's ghost was one of them.

ODDLY ENOUGH

Fate constructs memory in unforeseen ways. Given a certain compression of circumstances, a give-and-take honesty, a modicum of good cheer and sociability, and if you are able to embrace each other's take on life, you can learn quite a lot about a person in a short period of time. Late one morning, just a week after I had arrived in Churchill and set up in the motel, I stopped by Helen's room. I had not seen her that morning at breakfast at the Churchill Hotel, already an unusual absence since we had begun a routine of meeting for breakfast from day one. I knocked on her door and heard a weak "Come in." I opened the door and saw Helen curled up on the bed, clutching her stomach. She looked pale and there was a white film along her lips. She was fully dressed, including her green parka with plaid lining and what she told me was her favorite item of clothing, black buckle-up galoshes she had bought in Halifax. The shades were drawn; the sedatives Helen took sometimes made her eyes excruciatingly sensitive to light. "You okay?" I asked.

"I have stomach cancer," she said. She said it matter-of-factly. "So, there, now you know." I might have expected something else here. Some further explication. Even some judgment of my blank expression. But I soon realized that unembroidered self-assessment was an expertise of Helen's. She closed her eyes a moment, took a drink of water. "Rub my feet, will you?" she then said. "Sit and listen to the CBC for as long as you like, okay?" In discussing novels, Helen appreciated when a plot unfolded or a truth was revealed by indirection. This was paradoxical. Because in her own life, in conversations, she did not suffer indirectness. "Come to think of it, an hour listening to the radio will do."

I do not, here, want the fact of her cancer to import sentimentality into these recollections. Helen, I am convinced, would have despised that, chastised me for doing so even unwittingly. She would, I believe, have considered it a failure of character. In a letter she wrote, "I hate that my illness put such boundaries on elation." That sentence—! Given what was no doubt her mind-boggling pain and frustration, that sentence so characteristically bespoke Helen's writerly self. Elegant in restraint.

Upon her own arrival in Churchill, Helen had immediately set up a routine. She worked with Mark Nuqac all morning as her stamina allowed, beginning directly after breakfast. That is, if Mark was available—he was unreliable in this regard—taping, transcribing, discussing the Noah stories. Now and then I sat with Helen in Mark's cramped kitchen, with children and adults coming and going, this cousin or that, tea or coffee being prepared, potatoes being fried, the radio on, and on certain occasions such a pervasive air of distraction that it was difficult to imagine getting any translation work done, though Helen was stringent in her attempt to keep things on track. (Domestic chatter, radio music, and, in one instance, a child jumping on a bed with

squeaky springs is background noise on several tapes of my
own working sessions with Mark.) But more often than not,
Helen visited Mark on her own, and early on Mark informed me he preferred it that way. My own work with
Mark was altogether a less predictable arrangement. Mark
really kept me on my toes with scheduling, seeing that he
didn't much want to work with me at all, or did so grudg-
ingly. We might work all afternoon and late into the night,
and subsequently not work for three or four days on end. "I
know where to find you," he was fond of saying. In Mark
and his wife Mary's house food was always offered. (Mark
liked snacking on chunks of raw carrot or boxed breadsticks
with peanut butter. Also, he enjoyed black coffee with half a
dozen teaspoons of sugar.) But Helen's appetite—her ability,
that is, to keep down food—was meager. Her personal phar-
macy was always close at hand, eight or nine vials of pills
were either on her night table or stuffed into her parka
pockets or backpack. And as for generally bearing up, over
tea one morning she said, "Despite my medical circumstances, most days I don't feel life is rushing by, oddly
enough."

THE NOAH STORIES

Indelibly, every mental snapshot I retain of Churchill contains a raven or a group of ravens; the same with my dreams of Churchill. Ravens simply crowd into the picture. The proper terminology, I believe, is "a parliament of ravens." (It is "a murder of crows.") Ravens on the taiga, on the tundra, on the ground, in the black spruce of the bogs. Ravens along the railroad tracks. Ravens at the grain silos, out at the granary ponds, along the river. Then there is a kind of slapstick comedy one sees: raven dive-bombing polar bears foraging at the Churchill garbage dump, or nipping at a bear's genitals as it lolls on its back along the rocky beach of Hudson Bay.

There were two ravens as a greeting party when I stepped off the airplane on my first day at Churchill. Helen had arrived on August 22; I had arrived on August 27. Helen had taken the "Muskeg Express" train up from Winnipeg. My pilot's name was Driscoll Petchey (I used this name for a pilot in a novel, *The Haunting of L.*, set partly in Churchill), a real chatterbox. Setting my one suitcase on the ground, Petchey said, "Good luck every minute from now on," then walked ahead of me to the airstrip's small office.

Mark Nuqac's nephew Thomas drove me to the Beluga Motel. Not more than ten minutes after unpacking, there was a knock on the door. I opened it and there stood Helen.

"I have a very Japanese face, as you can see," she said, "but I'm English on my mother's side."

"What's your name? Why did you knock on my door?"

Helen was dressed in her green parka, a black turtleneck sweater underneath, blue jeans, those galoshes buckled to the top. Her black hair was tied up in back; she also had a kind of topknot, just on the very top of her head, which made me almost laugh. Stray hairs spilled out from the knot like a fountain.

"I'm Helen Tanizaki," she said, taking my hand in hers and shaking it. She let go of my hand and said, "Come on, I'll take you over to see Mark. He's in a very bad mood. He can't wait to meet you."

"Just a minute. How did you even know I was assigned to work with him? With Mr. Nuqac."

"Because I'm working with him, too. He mentioned you. Then you got here."

"You're working with him—in what sense?"

"Same as you, as it turns out."

"Same as me how?"

"Well, it's my understanding—am I mistaken?—that you're going to try and translate some of Mark's stories. And you've been hired by some museum or other. And that's why you're here."

"Correct."

"So—you are translating into English, right?"

"Yes."

"Me, I'm translating the same stories into Japanese. For a journal, and later possibly for a book."

"Nobody told me this would be the situation."

"Me either, Howard Norman."

"Mr. Nuqac had to agree to it, though."

"Of course. It was his idea."

"Why would he do that?"

"For one thing, he makes twice the money."

She shook her head side to side, as though I was the most naïve person on earth. "Okay, ready?"

"Yes."

"Put on your coat, then."

When we arrived at the small shacklike house Mark had borrowed for his stay in Churchill (Mark and his wife, Mary, had arrived from Eskimo Point via Winnipeg, where Mary had had a minor operation in the hospital), Helen said, "This part of town is called 'the Flats.'" The Flats was where some of the original parts of Churchill still remained; one brochure, or reference guide, said, "If you want to see how the Indians used to live in Churchill [referring mainly to the Cree], go have a look," euphemistic, I suppose, for declaring this area a kind of shantytown. My knock on the door was answered by Mary, who announced, without being asked, that Driscoll Petchey was, as we spoke, flying Mark the short distance to Padlei "to visit some cousins."

I killed time for two days, sizing up the town of Churchill, eating breakfast and dinner with Helen at the Churchill Hotel, going for walks carrying a rifle borrowed from Thomas, "in case of bears." When Helen told me that Mark had returned, I walked over to finally meet him. We did not shake hands; we just nodded hello. Mary just stood there observing this interaction without the slightest look of surprise.

"Okay, I've met you," Mark said. "The museum already sent some money. Ask Helen, here, when to see me. We can start working pretty soon, eh?" It was clear I was then to leave, which I did. I ate dinner with Helen at 7 p.m. at the Churchill Hotel, arctic char, potatoes, thawed vegetables, coffee. Just like every other night so far.

Here is a drawing of Churchill Helen made for me:

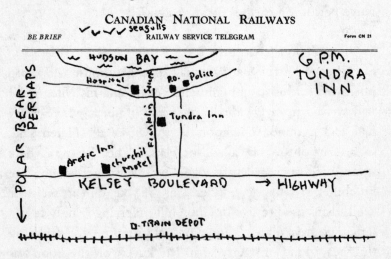

As I have mentioned, Mark referred to his stories as "my Noah stories." Generally, they each had these four things in common:

1. Noah's Ark drifts into Hudson Bay as winter is fast approaching.
2. Inuit villagers offer a bargain, or strongly suggest that Noah give up some of his unusual animals—and/or planks of wood from the ark—in exchange for their keeping Noah's family alive through the winter.

3. Noah refuses; said refusal engenders all manner of incident and repercussion.
4. After the spring ice-break-up, the ark sinks. Noah (and whichever members of his family who have survived) is sent packing southward on foot.

Ancient Inuit life so vividly animated in the Noah stories was, to say the least, hand-to-mouth. Fish had to be caught on a daily basis, seals or bears had to be killed as often as possible simply for people to exist. Not only can one read nineteenth-century ethnographic accounts or explorers' journals to get a sense of all this (keep in mind that Mark said his stories were "from Bible times," though we never discussed what he meant exactly), but of course traditional Inuit folktales are full of hardships. Hunting journeys were long, arduous, fraught with anxieties—and no doubt replete with joy, laughter, altruistic purpose, and the highest level of engagement with the physical and spiritual world—and, as often as not, unsuccessful. Starvation was not uncommon.

So: along comes a huge wooden boat full of elephants, giraffes, zebras, all sorts of curious, substantial-looking beasts. In a world of either feast or famine, imagine the sight to Inuit people as they looked up from their kayaks or sleds (as they do in Mark's stories) of such potentially grand meals in the making.

Ethnologists use the phrase "first contact stories" as a category of old-time narrative which depicts the exact moment in history when indigenous peoples first laid eyes on—spoke with, traded with, fought with, fled from—Europeans. The Noah stories, I think, basically fit that description. I asked

Mark Nuqac about this. I said, "Were there any white people up here before Noah showed up?"

Mark said, "No."

THE ARK IS TOO LOUD

One day at the beginning of winter, a big wooden boat was caught in the ice. The same day, a feared shaman showed up. This shaman walked directly into the village. "Did you invite that boat here?" he said.

"No," the villagers said. "We don't know why it's here."

"I like to sleep on the ice," the shaman said. "I like to sleep near seal breathing-holes."

"We know that."

"There's loud noises—animal barks, grunts, snores, shouts, yelps—coming from that boat. The boat is keeping me awake. Seals have the same complaint—they like to sleep on the ice, too."

In a short while winter arrived. The sea was covered with ice.

"You go out and stop the noise," the shaman said. "Go out there and stop it. Or else I'll cram your village—everybody, everything—down a seal breathing-hole. I can't sleep."

With this, some village men walked out over the ice to the boat. They shouted up, "Whose boat is this?"

"It's mine—my name is Noah," a man shouted down. "This is my wife—this is my son—this is my daughter." His family stood there now.

"What's this boat called in your language?"

"An ark," this Noah said.

"*Why does it make so much noise?*"

"*It's full of animals,*" Noah said.

"*We can smell them all the way into our village—are they tasty, what do they taste like, are they good to eat, will you share some with us?*" a man said.

"*No-no-no-no-no-no-no-no!*" said Noah.

"*What?*"

"*No!*" said Noah.

"*Why are you here?*"

"*I got lost.*"

"*Can you sleep with all that noise nearby?*"

"*No,*" said Noah. "*No,*" said Noah's wife. "*No,*" said Noah's daughter. "*No,*" said Noah's son.

"*Look out there on the ice,*" a villager said. "*What do you see?*"

"*A man asleep on the ice. Now he's woken up,*" Noah said.

"*Well, that man has big powers—and he's angry at your ark. He can't sleep. The ark is too loud. That man—if the ark stays loud—will cram our village through a seal breathing-hole. If the ark stays loud, that man will probably turn all of your animals inside out.*"

"*Nobody can do such things,*" Noah said.

"*You are wrong,*" a village man said.

"*Here's what you should do,*" another man said to Noah. "*Give us a few animals to eat. Give us a few planks of wood to make a fire with. Then give all the rest of the animals to that man—the shaman—and he'll cram them all through a seal breathing-hole. Then he'll be able to sleep. Then he won't turn the animals inside out, and he won't kill you, either.*"

Noah said, "No."

The villagers walked over to the shaman. "I can't sleep," he said.

The villagers sat next to him. When they sat down, the ark began making a lot of loud noises! "The man named Noah, there on the boat, won't make the noise stop," a village man said.

With this, the shaman flew to the top of the ark. "Your boat is too loud," he said. He took up Noah's wife and flew her around. They traveled. They came back. "Give up those animals," the shaman said.

"No!" said Noah.

The shaman took Noah's daughter and slipped with her through a seal's ice breathing-hole. They were gone for a few days. When they came back, Noah's daughter said, "Father, I don't want to do that again. Give up the animals."

"No," Noah said.

The shaman climbed onto the ark. He turned Noah's son inside out—some seagulls flew and plucked up the guts and insides, and flew off. Then the shaman turned each of the animals below deck on the ark inside out. He put them on deck—ravens and gulls flocked in—all the guts and insides were plucked up.

The shaman went out and lay down next to a seal breathing-hole. He fell asleep.

When the ice-break-up arrived, the shaman pried off a lot of planks. He gave a few to the village. He flew off carrying many ark planks. The ark sank away.

Noah and his family were taken into the village. They lived there much of the summer, Noah, Noah's wife, Noah's daughter.

One day, they wrapped themselves in the dried skins of some animals the shaman had turned inside out, and set out on foot in the southerly direction. There wasn't an ark in Hudson Bay again.

DRIFTWOOD

Local knowledge of Inuit births as it pertained to Mark Nuqac's generation is largely hearsay, though there are some frequently reliable church and missionary records, too. As far as I could find out, Mark's own parents were born near Baker Lake around 1890. Near the beginning of my time in Churchill Mark insisted that he was born in 1912, though near the end of my visit he mentioned that he was born in 1915.

Four main groups of Mark's extended community, or tribe, *Caribou Eskimo* (Inuit), were recognized by the Fifth Thule Expedition of 1921–24, led by the famous explorer-naturalist Knud Rasmussen, whose report was published in 1930. Mark claimed to have seen Rasmussen when he, Mark, was a boy. Neither Helen nor I believed him, but if one studies the demographics and calendar of Rasmussen's travels, it could have been true. Anyway, the designated groups are *Qairnirmiut, Hantiqtuurmiut, Harvaaqturrumiut, Paalirmiut*. Later, a fifth group, *Ahiarmiut*, to the southwest on the upper Maguse and Kazan Rivers, was recognized. Mark of course made claims for "first contact" in biblical times, but written records place first contact with white people in the eighteenth century, with the founding of

Churchill. A famous summer trading center was Akiliniq on the northwest side of Beverly Lake, where driftwood had drawn Inuit people from great distances.

Mark Nuqac remembered searching for driftwood there as a child. Here is part of the transcript of a conversation I had with Mark one evening in his kitchen. The subject was driftwood.

HN: You mentioned yesterday that you gathered driftwood at Akiliniq.

MN: Yes, I said that. Yes.

HN: With your family?

MN: Children ran along. Older people walked. Looking for driftwood. One summer we found a lot of pieces on the same morning.

HN: And it made for good fires?

MN: Dried out. Yes.

HN: Thank you for telling me. You look as if—. You look like you want to stop talking about this.

MN: One time something from a (capsized?) ship washed up. That caused a problem, a quarrel.

HN: About what had washed up? The quarrel.

MN: "I found it!" "No, it was me, I found it!" "I found it!" "No, no, no!" We were children.

HN: What was it—what had washed up?

MN: There was a lot of driftwood, too. But this was (*looks to his wife for the right word in English*)—a carved wooden face. From the—"

HN: —bow. The bow of a ship. The very front, where all the wind and sea spray flies up.

MN: Someone from a museum was up here. He heard us describe it. It was a woman's face. He said it was very old, probably.

HN: In what condition was it?

MN: Condition?

HN: You could see clearly that it was a woman's face?

MN: The schooner—the old ship—it went down. The woman's face was let go. It traveled to Akiliniq. My brothers and me found it. We were running around shouting, "Look at that! Look at that! Look at the old face!" That was a wonderful thing.

HN: Do you know where it is today?

MN: That is what the person from the museum asked me.

HN: Do you know where it is? I'd like very much to see it someday.

MN: Nobody kept it. We didn't keep it. But before we dried it and chopped it up—a lot was rotted out, but some could be saved—before that, we looked at it a long time. "I found it!" "No, I found it!" (*Laughing.*) "No—!"

HN: I'd like to have seen it.

MN: I'd like to see it again myself.

HN: How big was it?

MN: Two—three, of that stove, there. (*Points to the cast-iron potbelly stove.*) It was at Akiliniq. How could we carry it back? We chopped it up. How could you get the big carved face—very large—wooden face—the nose gone—all the way back? But when we got home we told everyone. We described it.

NOAH WOULD NOT GIVE UP
EVEN A SPLINTER

It was almost winter. But the water had not turned to ice yet. After one storm a piece of driftwood was seen out at sea. The villagers gathered together and pointed at it. "It's on top of a wave now," one shouted. "It's disappeared now! It's on top of a wave now!" But that piece of driftwood didn't tumble in. "I hope we can have one more driftwood-fire before winter," a man said.

The next day, a storm. No driftwood. The next day, a storm— no driftwood. The next day, a storm—no driftwood. The next day someone shouted, "Look—out there!" Everyone saw a big wooden boat on top of a wave.

A storm hit hard. It was windy and there was sleet. When the storm ended, some villagers went looking for driftwood. No driftwood. But they found an animal washed up on the rocks. "What is that?" a man asked.

"It's not a seal," another man said. "It's not a polar bear. It's not—It's not—It's not—" People were confused.

"It's not a whale," another villager said. The animal had a very long neck. It was very tall. It had yellow skin and black spots. "No, that's not a seal," a woman said. In a short while every villager had gone out to look at this animal.

"It must have escaped from the wooden boat," a man said. "Where else could it have come from?"

"Some of you haul it back out there," another woman said.

It took a lot of men to do this. They lay the tall animal across their kayaks. Paddling was not easy. There were rough waves and the spotted animal tilted the kayaks and kept them dangerously low

*in the water. When they got to the big wooden boat, a man shouted
up, "Hey—hey there!"*

*On deck appeared a man. He was standing next to a tall ani-
mal with black spots. It had a long neck. Its skin was yellow—not
paled by drowning, either. It had small horns. "Hey, there's another
one!" a man shouted. "I wonder how it tastes?"*

"What do you want?" the man shouted down.

"We've brought this dead animal back."

"It fell off my ark."

"What's that?"

"It's what my boat is called."

"What's your name?"

"Noah."

"What's this animal called?"

"A giraffe."

"Where you come from do you eat it?"

"Not my family."

"Is your family with you?"

"Yes—my wife. My son. My daughter."

"I bet they're inside the ark eating a giraffe."

The villagers in kayaks all laughed.

"No—no—there's only this one left alive," said Noah.

*"Winter is coming in fast. You'll be without food. You better
think about eating that giraffe."*

"No," said Noah.

*"Well, the one lying across these kayaks is dead. We don't eat
dead animals. Ravens might—foxes might, if the carcass is frozen.
Crows do that, gulls do that."*

"I don't want the dead giraffe," said Noah.

With that, the villagers pushed the giraffe into the sea. "Giraffe-sank-away," a man said.

It became winter. It was snowing. The ark was trapped in ice out there. Great hummocks of sea ice pushed up against it. Snow fell on the giraffe. Snow fell on Noah. In the village, people said, "Hey, Noah and his family must be hungry. If we have luck in hunting, let's bring them a seal." It was agreed. Some hunters walked out over the ice. They bent over seal breathing-holes. They caught many seals. All at once the dogs began to bark—all across the ice—echoes of dog barks—over there—over there—and the seal hunters looked around. "Hey—look there!" one shouted. Then from a different place on the ice men saw the other tall spotted giraffe walking out over the ice! Its long legs were not good for this. It collapsed and fell, it got up, it fell, it slid around. "Giraffe-on-the-ice," a hunter said.

"Let's get it!" another said.

So the men hunted the giraffe. When they got up close they threw spears and gaffing hooks and killed the giraffe. They fed some of it to their dogs. The dogs ate what they were given right away. The men hauled the rest back to their village. People there looked at the strange hooves. People ate some of the giraffe but didn't like it.

"Let's say thanks to Noah anyway," a woman said.

"He didn't give us this food," a hunter said. "We got it."

"His family must be starving," a woman said. "Bring him some of this animal, at least." So the hunters dragged the giraffe haunches out to the ark. "Hey, Noah!" one shouted out. "Here's some food to get you by for a while!"

"No!" Noah called down. "I see pieces of spotted hide still attached. We don't want it!"

"Noah, give us a plank of wood, we'll get you through the winter," a hunter said. "We'll show you how to chisel through the ice

for fishing. We'll show you how to lean over a seal breathing-hole. Just give us a plank of wood."

"No!" Noah shouted in anger. When he shouted, he slid his hand across the rail of his ark. "Oh! Oh!" The villagers saw he had got a splinter in his thumb.

"Hey, Noah," a man said, "Just give us that splinter! We'll get you and your family through winter. Hey, come on! We can get that splinter out for you. We get splinters out all the time. Come on, it's just a tiny piece of wood. We get bone splinters out, other sorts . . . fish-bone splinters. We can spark a fire from just that splinter. Come on, we'll climb up and get that splinter out!"

Noah walked to the rail. He saw a villager climbing up. Noah struck this man with a long stick with bristles at the end. The man fell to the ice. "Hey—hey!" the man said. "Noah, what did you hit me with?"

"A broom," said Noah.

"Well, a bristle stuck in my face. I'm going to try and spark a fire from it!"

"Go away!" said Noah.

"Let us have the broom," said a man, "we'll get you through winter. Otherwise you'll starve."

"No, I sweep the ark with it every day," said Noah.

"Give us the broom, you won't have to sweep anymore!"

"No!"

The man Noah had struck with the broom said, "All right— winter can have you." The villagers all went home.

After the ice-break-up, some men paddled out to the ark. It was floating now, turning in slow circles, a lot of pieces of ice were still bumping against it. The men climbed onto the ark. "Hey—hey— Noah!" they shouted. They didn't hear any voice. They saw a lot of animal bones—all sizes—no animals. Then they saw Noah. He was lying down curled up. He was weeping. He was wearing a coat made of faded yellow skin with black spots. "One thumb splinter —one broom—one plank of wood," a man said, "it was a very tough winter. Where's your wife? Where's your son? Where's your daughter?"

"They ate the broom bristles and died," said Noah.

Some men pried up some planks and put them in their kayaks. They felt the ark begin to sink away. It was windy. It was raining hard. "Let's get this Noah to the village," a man said.

They took Noah and the planks to the village. They built a fire. Noah sat next to it. They fed him and kept him alive. He lived with them all summer and through the next winter. A few times they caught him walking out onto the ice. "He sees the ghosts of his family," a man said. It was true. Noah made a new broom and swept around. He ate, he swept, and every once in a while people caught him out on the ice. They brought Noah back.

One day in the middle of winter someone shouted, "It's Noah— he's out on the ice again! Hey—what are you doing?"

"I'm following my wife—look—up ahead—she's lost," he said.

One day later that winter someone shouted, "Hey—look! Noah, what are you doing out on the ice?"

"I'm following my daughter—look!—up ahead—she's lost," he said.

On another day, Noah said, "I'm out on the ice because— look!—up ahead—it's my son—he's lost. I'm going after him to help."

Each time the villagers would tie Noah up with gut string and haul him back sliding over the ice. When they untied him in the village, he ate and got some strength back. Then he swept with the broom. He seldom slept. He swept and the villagers heard that sound. "No ark—but he sweeps," a woman said.

When next time the ice-break-up arrived, the villagers decided that Noah had lived with them long enough. They went with him in the southerly direction. Then they gave him packets of food and sent him on his way. Planks from the ark washed up for a lot of summers. Not every time after a storm, but still there was driftwood, driftwood—driftwood. From that ark.

THE STUFF OF NOAH'S CHARACTER

Mark Nuqac was about five feet four inches tall, stocky. I thought he had a dignified bearing. Helen told me that Mark had never been to a dentist (how did such subjects come up in their conversation? "He joked about it," Helen said); his teeth were bad, the best front ones crooked, one of those seemed to push slightly at his lip. He had close-cropped black hair. His roundish face was most deeply etched on his forehead, a veritable light brown earth-map of latitude lines. He had pronounced "crow's-feet" wrinkles at each eye, a broad aspect to his cheekbones, a taut, thin-lipped smile, a notched and scarred left ear, the result of a sled-dog bite when he was a boy. Though he generally held a solemn expression, focused, not preoccupied, his face could truly brighten—I witnessed this every time Helen stepped into his kitchen. He was both gruff and cordial in equal measure, it seemed, to his wife, Mary, whom he had been married to for forty-six years. Mary did not at all strike me as long-suffering; as much as I understood their occasional bickering, she gave as well as she got, and I never saw them apart, except once, when Mark and Helen were walking by the river, or when Mark, with somewhat alcohol-emboldened entitlement, took it upon himself to stumble into Helen's motel room, "unannounced," as Helen put it, and hold forth on this or that subject. More than once Mary had to fetch him back home; Mary and Helen had a cordial relationship—Helen spent considerable time with Mary Nuqac, and Mary provided certain clarifications about any number of sentences, let alone entire stories, Helen was translating.

Mary Nuqac was a few inches shorter than Mark. She had reddish brown skin, darker than Mark's, and her eyes were darker brown, too. Her rather long face—most notably the sides—was mottled with age spots, like a map of islands. Her hair, gray-flecked black, was cut close except for one braid bobby-pinned in a haphazard coil at the back of her head. Neither Helen nor I learned where Mary was born, but she once allowed that she had spoken a different dialect of Inuit when she was a child. She married Mark when she was seventeen; I was surprised, for reasons having to do with Mark's cynicism toward "church," that they had had "a Christian wedding," and that both Mark and Mary had indeed been baptized. "I still don't mind church," she said. You definitely could call Mary "stout"; she wore sweaters too small for her physical stature, and often they were buttoned unevenly. She wore tennis shoes and sweat socks, and a few times she had on what she called "nurse shoes"—her sister, Maude, was a nurse in a small clinic near Lake Winnipegosis, Manitoba, and had sent her these white shoes in her size. Mary could read and write in English, and for some years clerked in a store. I did not get to know Mary well at all, but on one occasion we had a somewhat lengthy conversation in English, which centered on the Beluga Motel's plumbing. Years earlier, Mary had watched the original plumbing being installed, and went into great detail about how people went every day to observe the motel's construction from the ground up. It was a rather odd topic, I thought, but I was happy to be speaking with her alone; she ended by confessing that she had regretted not becoming a plumber. "I saw how everything fit," she said. "I even asked a fellow if I could help out, but he didn't want me to. I could've helped out—no question." (One other thing: that was an oft-used phrase, "no question"—it meant *no question about it.*)

Helen promised to send Mary a kimono; Mary had seen women wearing kimonos in a *National Geographic* magazine and thought their colors and design were beautiful. Mary had a *National Geographic* map of the world thumbtacked to the kitchen wall and had circled Japan with a black crayon.

Mary and Mark had had five children. Their second son was lost to suicide; a daughter, born with a weak heart, died of complications from scarlet fever at age two. A daughter was living in Winnipeg; a son lived in Vancouver and was married to a Chinese woman. Their eldest son had died at forty of natural causes in Padlei. If the face, as Akutagawa wrote, is "the registry of all we experience," then I could fully imagine that Mary could decipher much of Mark's emotional biography each time she looked at him—and, no doubt, Mark could "read" Mary's face for joys and griefs as well. One morning, when I saw Mark holding Mary's face with his hands, massaging it as if to slightly realign the past, it struck me as some age-old form of literacy, the reading of a husband's or wife's face, because Mark was concentrating the way a person reads and rereads a particularly astonishing passage in a book.

I want to describe a typical afternoon of working with Mark Nuqac, not that there was such a thing. Typical, I mean. Each working session was different in small and large ways, subtle or outlandish, and each day we never really got along that well. On October 4 Mark seemed quite willing, in fact insisted on speaking about the character of Noah himself. For one thing, he informed me of the "origin"—I took this in part to imply a source of inspiration—for the story "Why Woolly Mammoths Decided to Flee Underground." (My title—Mark did not title his stories.)

I could not for the life of me figure out why Mark set aside his highly impersonal manner to speak about the chief antagonist of his Noah stories, Noah himself, but I was grateful for it. For it was otherwise all too clear that the wider context of our work together—that he was paid, as it were, for being a raconteur (he once emphatically remarked, "You can't put these stories into a museum, even though you work for one")—made him somewhat uneasy. Helen pointed out that the Japanese language was so outside of Mark's experience that having his stories reside in Japanese might, in ways we perhaps could not fully comprehend, be less distasteful. "He likes the *sound* of Japanese more than the sound of English," Helen said. "He asks me to speak it all the time. He closes his eyes and listens. There's nothing *rational* about any of this—it's just the way it is. He doesn't much enjoy speaking English, either, have you not noticed?

Maybe it's because you're—what does he say—European? White—whereas I'm not, completely. Some sort of affinity there perhaps. It's impossible to figure it all out, to have it make perfect sense. There's many parts to it, Howard Norman."

I suppose it took a few weeks not to feel hurt by Mark's intolerances, his edginess, at times his outright hostility—I took it all quite personally, and I brooded out loud about it to Helen. "It's not that I'm a rival for his affections," she said. "I'm a woman, he's a big flirt, he says very sexual things to me, sexual innuendos, sexual jokes. He clearly enjoys his own crudeness of that sort. Mary says, 'My husband likes to get your goat.' I can't imagine where she picked that phrase up. I'd like to know, actually."

"Look, Helen, I'm not very good at this work yet. That's got to be crystal clear to Mark. He's impatient with me, and I can tell there's disappointment. It's all over his face. He must be thinking, 'They've sent an incompetent.' If I'm honest about it, I think it'd take me twenty-five years to get this language. And even then—"

"Now look who's feeling sorry for himself. It's a beautiful language, though. You must feel that."

"Of course I do. So far I speak it like a kindergartner."

"Not quite up to that, I'm afraid."

"Besides, Helen, you just have this facility. An ear for it."

"I think those lessons you had in Toronto served you well, though."

"I bet you dream in Inuit. Does that ever happen?"

"Does what happen, people in my dreams speaking Inuit?"

"Yes."

"Only when the people in my dreams *are* Inuit."

"Funny."

"You can't expect to be a native speaker *unless* you put in twenty-five years. In that you are quite correct. I mean, look around you: there's a lot of young people up here who don't have the language, right? So even not every *native* is a native speaker."

"I'm just worrying these translations to death, that's my problem."

"They're beautiful stories, though, don't you think?"

Back to October 4. I spent the better part of the day in Mark's kitchen. Except for a brief lapse into whiskey, Mark and I stuck to drinking coffee. I had the big tape recorder on his splintery wooden table. Mary served us each a bowl of chicken noodle soup out of a can for lunch. When we finished our soup, I took out my spiral notebook and pen. (Helen had taped to its cover an illustration of Noah on the ark, big billowing clouds threatening rain, Noah's wife with a worried look on her face—Helen said she'd cut it out of a children's collection of Bible stories.) "Go ahead, use the machine," Mark said. Ravens were squawking loudly—also emitting clicks as if speaking in Morse code—outside the house. I switched on the reel-to-reel and Mark started right in—his voice was raspy, he had a sore throat, he was sucking on a Smith Brothers cherry-flavored cough drop.

"They find woolly elephants in the ice," he said. "Bet you didn't know that, eh?"

"Mastodons, I think they call them," I said. "I don't actually know if woolly mammoths and mastodons are the same thing, but they might be. You call them 'woolly elephants' sometimes, right?"

Mark set on the table a magazine article he'd clipped out. It contained photographs showing paleontologists on scaffolding. They were excavating a mastodon from a wall of ice, using ice picks and what looked like welder's torches. One of the paleontologists had a belt festooned with scrub brushes and toothbrushes. The mastodon loomed ghostlike behind the partly transparent surface, which was like smoked glass—one of the mastodon's curved tusks had broken off and floated a tusk's-length from the hollow-eyed shaggy face.

"Look, here," Mark said, pointing to some men at the base of the glacier. "Those are Eskimo. I don't know where from. The article don't say."

I looked at the photographs and read the captions. When Mark figured I'd had enough time with them, he put the article in his front trouser pocket. "When they got the animal out," he said—he had obviously had the article read to him a number of times, since Mark himself could not read—"it smelled very bad, but they tossed some meat to the dogs! Now, it must've not been completely rotten, eh, 'cause they wouldn't want to poison dogs." Mark looked incredulous, at the phenomenon of still-edible meat from the age of mastodons—!

"Do you remember when you first heard about Noah?" I said, trying to not sound like I was participating in some sort of academic-style Q&A.

"I first heard about Noah because I sat in church a few times," he said without hesitation. "I asked my father about this Noah. He told me some things. He told me the Bible story, what a lot of people believe."

Mark's spoken English was definitely stilted, he was never less than tentative with it. You could almost feel the physical process of translation, the delay, the search for words, the inadequate vocabulary, brilliant storyteller that he was. I certainly identified with the essential difficulty; after all, I felt quite inept in Mark's language. When he spoke, even in our informal dialogues, he often articulated a thought in Inuit first, then did his best in English—in other words, he became his own translator out loud. Helen said that Mark had a "slurring English," by which she meant that the thick-tongued consonant sound of Inuit was somewhat reprised in Mark's English pronunciations. (Several ethnographic reports—and one explorer's journal—from the nineteenth century attest to the fact that the neighboring Cree Indians thought Inuit around Hudson Bay sounded like they had "stones in their mouths when they talked.") One morning I outright apologized for my poor spoken Inuit. Mark said, "Okay—well. When you and Helen leave, I will earn twenty-four hundred dollars Canadian for this work," a guarded, elliptical reply, which I took in part to mean suffering a linguistic fool such as I was truly earning his keep. Which I fully agreed with.

Hard to know for sure, but it felt like Mark was enjoying our discussion, perhaps especially speaking about his father, whom he clearly loved and admired. "My father knew the Bible pretty good—he knew the Bible stories pretty good," Mark said. Out came a small flask of whiskey, which had an eagle etched on it. It looked just like a flask I had seen for sale in the Hudson's Bay Company store. "My father liked going to the church talks—"

"The sermons?" I said.

"The sermons. He used to sit in the front pew and laugh out loud. He'd say to the clergy fellow—'Hey, hey, get it right, get it right. That's not how it happened!' Like with this Noah fellow—my father got his own way to understand it, eh?"

"So, you heard some of the Noah stories from your father?"

"A few. Not too many. But most of 'em came from—" He pointed to the side of his head, then took two healthy swigs.

I immediately poured myself more coffee and said, "More coffee, Mark? I think it'd be a good idea."

He screwed on the top, which was connected by a necklace-thin chain soldered to the main body of the flask. He set the flask on the counter near the sink. "Okay, more coffee for me, I guess," he said.

"The story of the woolly mammoths just disappearing under the ice—you heard that one from your father?"

"Yes, go ahead, write that down. He watched me write, *Mark heard woolly mammoth story first from his father.* Staring at my notebook a silent moment, Mark finally said, "I'd read the Bible, I guess. But I wouldn't learn to read just to do that!" He laughed. "My grandchildren read their books to me, eh? That's a very nice thing. That's a very good thing."

"Is it"—I searched for the right word and couldn't find

it—"*strange*, hearing your stories read back to you, in English?"

"I think my grandchildren might like to read them. They like to read Eskimo stories in books. Other kinds, too. They go to a library."

I showed him the depiction of Noah on the cover of my notebook. "This picture of Noah is from a book for children," I said. "But how did anyone really know what he looked like?"

This, for some reason, made Mark laugh harder than I'd ever seen him laugh before or since.

"This Noah fellow—in all the stories—he's— (Mark used a phrase, which, with assistance from Helen and an early-twentieth-century vocabulary list, I learned meant, roughly, *lost his human bearing*).

"Yes, in your stories, Noah does seem very lost."

"He drifted lost up here, and when that happens, it is a hard thing. When I was a boy I often heard of people getting lost. Lots of ways to get lost, eh? Some people fell right through the ice. Others got caught—lost—in blizzards. That's how it was. I often heard about such things. You wait and try to think of a way out of it. You wait for some help to come along. Or you wait to die. Lost, eh? This Noah, I have him get lost in all my stories—'Where am I? Where am I?'—he don't know. He don't understand how to live up here, eh?"

"No, he doesn't."

"A little like *you*! You—hey, you remind me of this Noah fellow!" He drank some coffee.

To extend the metaphor, I was indeed adrift. First, not

knowing a language spoken in a household means in a basic
sense you are infantalized; you can't tell what people are saying about you, you are adrift in a constant haze of doubt, the
most familiar object (say a teapot) is unfamiliar until you
know how to refer to it in a simple sentence. Secondly, I was
adrift between occupations. I was constructing a frightfully
useless résumé: freelance articles on every subject imagina-
ble—I even wrote about polar bears for a Florida newspaper,
book reviews for a newspaper in Reykjavík—obtained a
small grant here and there to collect folklore in Nova Scotia,
was briefly in the employ of the World Wildlife Fund (to
help interview Chippewa and Cree Indians in Ontario and
Manitoba about the poaching and illegal export of bear liv-
ers for aphrodisiacs!), managed to get a high school lecture
now and then, wrote several narratives for children's films
about arctic animals. I was exhaustingly peripatetic. When
all the while I wanted to sit in a hotel room and write novels. That was my big secret. At the time I was definitely
without literary prospects. (Perhaps not surprisingly, the pro-
tagonist of my first novel, *The Northern Lights*, was named
Noah.) Thirdly, I was adrift between an absence of romance
and meeting my future wife, Jane, in 1981, though in
Churchill there was no way to foresee that I would have
such good fortune. Yet I knew I wanted a family of my own
someday. Most immediately, of course, I was adrift in the
desire—it felt like an enormous sea-of-desire—to comprehend as much about Helen Tanizaki as possible. To get my
human bearing in relation to Helen. Because she was dying;
this fact required that I more memorize her than slowly "get
to know" her—there was to be no *slowly* allowed.

"Maybe I am lost," I said to Mark, "but at least I'm working with you right here and now at this table, right? I'm asking for help all the time, right?"

"I'm happy to be paid, working with you."

"I know that."

"That's good. That's good."

"For instance, Mark, there's parts of the woolly mammoth story I need to listen to with you again, on the tape recorder, all right? Maybe five or ten times over again. I need help with it."

"Helen can help."

"Yes, she can, but I need to work with you on it more. What the museum is paying you for, remember?" I immediately regretted saying that.

I played the story and we worked on it for two hours; the notebook pages filled, we went through two more pots of coffee. Mary left the house twice, returning each time with something from the grocery store. Mark and I went outside for a piss a few times. It felt like a very productive day of work.

Then, toward suppertime, things went bitterly awry. Perhaps it was partly due to the exasperating work itself, no matter how much real progress was made; perhaps our ration of civility had been used up; there could have been any number of reasons. I had one more item to discuss with Mark, so I ventured forth. "Mark, when you say"—and I attempted to pronounce a passage in Inuit concerning the actual moment when the woolly mammoths are insulted by Noah and make the *decision* to flee underground (see "Why Woolly Mammoths Decided to Flee Underground," p. 62)—"does that mean that *one* woolly elephant went under the ice because it was insulted, or does it mean . . . ?"

I was startled by the suddenness with which Mark scraped his chair back, rose with a fierce look of indignation on his face, and walked into the bedroom and sat on the edge of the bed, his head hung like he had just received terrible news. Looking through the open doorway (there was in fact no door), I saw Mary sit next to Mark, all the while looking at me, offering two quick shrugs, *What happened?* Mary, I noticed, was wearing a brown button-down sweater over a pale yellow button-down sweater; the brown one looked to be directly buttoned to the yellow one, which was also buttoned its entire length. Mary turned off the radio, then spoke in low tones to Mark in their language. She must have convinced him of my best intentions, because Mark soon returned to the kitchen table. He sat down, sipped cold coffee without meeting my eyes. I grew quite anxious within this silence—it felt like a standoff, but over what, I had no idea. I too stared away.

But in a moment I began more or less studying Mark's face in its repose. Because now he didn't appear angry at all; he looked at ease, if anything, lost in thought, as though some sort of erasure of conflict had occurred. Still, he did not look at me. But then he caught me studying his face. I must have been holding a blank stare, because he said, "Are you—a—*hypnotist* fellow?"

"I apologize for staring, Mark. I think you mean that I looked *hypnotized.*"

Mary sat down at the table. "We had a hypnotism fellow up here to visit at schools one time," she said. "I mean to

Churchill, then up to Eskimo Point, a few other places, too. A magician—he was funny. He tried to hypnotize my sister. It didn't work."

Mark now imitated a metronome by tocking his pointer finger back and forth, then affected his own "hypnotized" blank expression, a man asleep with his eyes open. Outside of the formidable verbal comedy of incident and dialogue in his Noah stories, this brief miming was the boldest humor I'd yet to experience from Mark. (Helen said, "He's one of the funniest people I've ever met." We knew in Mark two different people. "He often makes me laugh. Perhaps you have to understand the language a bit more. Sorry.")

Helen simply walked into the house without knocking. Mark said, "Helen, my daughter—we were just telling this man, here, about something."

Helen kissed Mary on her forehead, kissed Mark on the top of his head. She looked at the flask. "Having fun?" she said to me.

"We've been working all day," I said.

"How did it go?" Helen said, directing her question to Mark.

"He caught a little," Mark said. He half whispered something to Mary; they both abruptly left the house.

"I feel like shit," Helen said. "Excuse my French."

"I don't suppose you'd want coffee. It tastes like mud with sugar in it."

"No thank you."

I shut off the reel-to-reel, closed my notebook, put the pen in my shirt pocket. "Well, that's that."

"Mark suddenly looked pissed," Helen said. "Why, do you suppose?"

"I really don't understand it," I said. "Things were going along nicely."

"How nicely, Howard Norman?"

"More nicely than usual."

"Of course, that's not saying much."

"Thanks, Helen."

She looked around the kitchen. "Oh, chicken noodle soup. The specialty of the house."

"I actually had a meal with Mark. I didn't care if it was canned soup or not. Things were going really well. We were going through a passage in that woolly mammoth story, you know the one."

"Indeed, I do know it. It absolutely explains why we won't be seeing any woolly mammoths on the horizon. It absolutely explains it."

"—and the mood changed."

"Mercurial, that man. Wouldn't you say?"

"Sure, that's it."

"But, look: you and Mark simply do not get on well at all. But I'm quite bored discussing the whys and where-fores of your situation. I wish to offer two words: *Boo hoo.* He sits with you most every day, doesn't he? Probably, you shouldn't expect much more than you're already getting from Mark. That's my word to the wise."

We sat a moment, not talking. Helen took a sip of my coffee and spit it out, "Pfwooo!" Spit it all over my trouser leg.

"Helen, you want to listen to the CBC after supper?"

"I'll have to type. But when I'm done, sure."

We did listen to the radio for quite a while. An opera, then a documentary about a Jewish Dutch cellist murdered during World War II, including testimonies from people who actually knew him. Then we talked awhile. As usual, we discussed our work with Mark, dissecting it from every possible angle. I guess I was still a bit bruised from what had occurred that afternoon; Helen picked up on this. "If it helps any," Helen said, "Mark asked me what I thought of your work and I said good things."

"Yeah, but what does Mark himself think? Do you know, really?"

"Next subject, please."

"Come on—consider it gossip. You know how much Mark loves gossip."

"He said you try very hard. He added that a baby fox tries very hard when it's learning to piss in the snow. But it often pisses on its own leg."

WHY WOOLLY MAMMOTHS DECIDED TO FLEE UNDERGROUND

I heard about Noah while sitting on a pew in church, but later, from an old man in our village, I found out what really happened.

Noah and his family were starving. By the time their ark had drifted up here, they had eaten many animals, but still there were a lot left. First, the ark drifted far north of Hudson Bay—far, far north, up where walrus live. One day the ark bumped up against an ice floe. Noah looked out and saw walrus on the ice. He some-

how managed to kill a walrus. He somehow managed to get more walrus on his boat, too. The Bible says two, two of each animal, but by the time Noah got here, his family was so hungry, he forgot all about two. He got as many walrus on the ark as he could. He got a few seals on the boat. Seagulls, too.

It was said that all the people drowned where Noah had come from—all of them! But up around here, there were many of us, many people.

The ark drifted into Hudson Bay. People saw it floating out there. They were curious. Some people quickly got into kayaks and paddled out.

"Hey, what kind of boat is this?" one hunter asked.

"What do you mean?" Noah said.

"What's it made of?"

"Wood."

"We get wood that washes up after a storm. Driftwood."

"Are you going to kill us?" Noah said.

"No."

"What is the best way to leave this place?"

"Go back to where you came from."

"I can't do that."

"Why?"

"I have to wait until God calls down and says it's okay."

"Who is that?"

"Who controls things here?"

"Many things—many spirits—different ones. Important ones."

"Not me—the one who controls things for me is back home."

"You're wrong."

"No."

"Yes. If you live here—the important spirits control you."

"Not me."

"You're wrong."

Then Noah threw some big handfuls of animal dung down at the people in their kayaks. They paddled off. The ark drifted out on Hudson Bay all night.

The next day people paddled out to the ark again.

"Hey, what's falling from the sky?" Noah said.

"Snow."

"I don't like it. It's cold."

"Ha-ha-ha-ha-ha!" the villagers all laughed up from their kayaks.

Noah threw big handfuls of dung down on them and they paddled away.

The next day, some hunters paddled out to the ark again.

"What's that animal taste like—is it good?" one hunter said.

"Which one?" said Noah.

"The one that has the long neck and spots."

"There's two of them," said Noah.

"Let us have one. We'll tell you how it tastes, good or bad."

"No," said Noah.

"If you visit a village you should give something. You have a lot of food-animals there. Give us one."

"No."

"Soon it will be snowing harder. Soon snow will cover everything. Soon ice will gather tightly around your boat."

"How do I get out of here?"

"You have to live here all winter."

Hearing this put Noah in a bad way. He looked angry. He shouted. He threw more handfuls of dung, but the people had backed up their kayaks already. "Come to our village and we will let you live with us all winter. Are you alone?"

"No, I have a wife. I have a son. I have a daughter."

"We'll find someone to marry each of those."

"Go away."

The hunters paddled back in the snowfall over the water. When it was snowing its hardest, that is when a woolly elephant came out and was walking around. Woolly mammoths were around, then, and this one was walking along the shore. Then the ice locked in the ark.

Ice locked in the ark and a woolly mammoth walked out to the ark. Everyone in the village saw this.

Some hunters got spears, ran out, and tried to cut off the woolly mammoth. They closed in on it. The woolly mammoth had three choices: it could keep walking fast away, it could turn on the hunters, it could climb onto the ark.

The woolly mammoth tried to climb onto the ark, but its tusks tore into the sides. Then it loosened from the ark and climbed up onto it. Some villagers went out and repaired the holes, covered them with stretched sealskins. Then they shouted up to Noah, "Look, we repaired your boat. Now, please give us that woolly mammoth. It can give us enough food for our whole village."

"No," said Noah. "I need it. I'll kill it and my family will eat it."

"You don't know how to eat a woolly mammoth!" a hunter said.

"Go away. Get out of here!"

The villagers went back home over the ice. They went hunting, they fished. Food was brought in and people didn't go hungry yet.

One day Noah showed up in the village. "We've run out of food," he said. "My family is hungry."

"Did you eat some more of the strange animals you travel with?"

"Yes, but others run from us when we approach, or fly up, or flee out over the ice."

"Yes, we've seen some run over the ice."

"Do you have some food for us?" Noah said.

"Do you know how to hunt seals through breathing-holes?"

"No."

"Do you know how to chisel a hole for ice fishing?"

"No."

"If another woolly mammoth climbs onto your boat, will you give it to us?"

"No."

Hearing this, some hunters poked spears at Noah. They did not stab into him. They only pushed him along the ice, all the way back to his ark. The hunters returned home.

Snow and sleet, more snow. It was deep into winter now. Then, one day, some villagers were out hunting woolly mammoths. They saw one. They began to chase it. They were almost close enough to throw spears when the woolly mammoth climbed onto the ark. The hunters were impressed, how woolly mammoths had learned how to climb onto an ark. This one did it on the first try! The hunters admired the woolly mammoth very much.

A hunter called up to Noah, "Give us the woolly mammoth!"

"No!" said Noah. "It's mine. I'll kill it and eat it."

Noah had made a spear. He stood near the woolly mammoth. He threw from close up and missed, which is hard to do, miss a woolly mammoth completely. The spear didn't even bounce off the woolly mammoth's hide!

The woolly mammoth fled the ark then. It ran off across the ice, out to other woolly mammoths. The woolly mammoths talked amongst themselves. Finally, they decided to live under the ground. They decided this so as not to be hunted improperly—to be insulted—by Noah. This is how Noah caused woolly mammoths to flee underground. The villagers never saw a woolly mammoth again.

All the rest of that winter, villagers left scraps of food for Noah and his family. Ptarmigan bones. Rotted seal flippers. Things picked out of fox droppings and polar bear droppings. Fish skulls and fish bones and dried-up fish tails. It got Noah's family through until the ice thawed.

When the ice thawed, the ark sank into the water. Some villagers paddled out and carried Noah and his family to the village in kayaks. Then they poked spears at them. "Go. Get out! Go in that direction!"

The villagers watched Noah and his family set out to the south. They carried a little food. When Noah and his family were no longer seen, the villagers went back to everything as it was before.

That is what happened.

LAST CONVERSATION WITH MARK, 1977

(Transcript)

MN: You leave on the train soon, eh?

HN: In a few days, yes.

MN: Helen with you?

HN: Yes.

MN: She will not be staying, then.

HN: No.

MN: Helen and me, we did a lot of good work, I'd say.

HN: She said that.

MN: Good.

HN: Thanks for all of your help, Mark. It meant a lot to me. It was important to me.

MN: Helen taught me a lot of Japanese words. Did you know that?

HN: No.

MN: Well, she did.

HN: As for your stories, I won't ever think of Noah—

MN: —oh, *him.*

HN: I won't ever think of Noah in the same way. The rest of my life.

MN: All he ever had to do was give up some animals and pry off a plank of wood.

HN: *You* didn't allow him to do that. In your stories, I mean.

MN: Noah didn't allow it.

HN: But they're your stories, Mark. So—

MN: I don't own them. I only tell them. (*Pause.*) When do you think I'll get the rest of my money for telling them?

HN: Soon. Let's say in two weeks. I'll see to it, Mark.

MN: Helen has already paid me.

HN: Yes, she told me.

MN: You liked the stories, eh?

HN: Very much. I was lucky to hear them.

MN: All that good plank-wood—

HN: —what?

MN: All he had to do was pry up a plank. Everybody would have got through winter.

A BAD THING IS ABOUT TO HAPPEN

One day some men came back from fishing. They said, "There's a big wooden boat out there!" Everyone in the village went down to look. They stood by the sea. "Yes, there it is." A group of men paddled out in kayaks to the boat.

It began to snow.

When they got to the boat, one shouted, "Hey—what kind of boat is this?"

"Go away!" a man shouted down.

"What's your name?"

"Noah!"

"Is your family with you?"

"Yes," said Noah. Then three people were standing next to him. "Here they are—my wife, son, and daughter."

"Noah," said a village man, "you should come to our village—now! A bad thing is about to happen."

"Go away."

"What's this big boat called, anyway?"

"An ark."

"Noah, leave this ark—a bad thing is about to happen."

"What's that smell?" a man said. "It's not seals."

"There's a lot of animals on my ark. After long travels on this boat, they stink."

"Throw them down to us. We'll kill them and eat them. What do they taste like?"

"My family doesn't eat them," this Noah said.

This caused a lot of talk amongst the villagers. "What? What? What?"

Then someone sniffed the air. "Hey! Hey—the stink is gone!"

Noah went below to look, and when he returned, he said, "The animals are gone. Somebody took them. A bad thing just happened."

"It has to be the shaman. He's been nearby some days now," a villager said.

"Why would he steal my animals?" said Noah.

"Because he doesn't want you here. He hates your ark. He's probably tasting a few of your animals right now, at the bottom of the sea, or maybe in a far place, behind some rocks. He'll never tell us what they taste like, either. He'll keep the animals for himself."

"What's falling from the sky?" asked Noah's wife.

"Snow—it's winter now," a man said.

"What will happen?" she said.

With this, winter arrived. The ark was stuck in the ice. Seals came up through breathing-holes out on the ice—you could hear them barking. Then someone shouted, "Look—!" and people saw all sorts of strange animals next to seal breathing-holes! Animals the villagers had never seen before—strange animals. "The shaman's hid them below the ice!"

"Bring me this man—this shaman," said Noah. "I'll sweep him down to the ice with my broom!" This made the villagers laugh very hard.

"You can't fight him," a man said. "He'll stab your broom straight through your heart—he'll do what he wants."

"How will I get my animals back?" Noah said.

"Offer the shaman some planks of wood—for a fire," a man said.

"No," said this Noah.

"Then you'll have to dive under the ice itself," a man said.

"No," said Noah.

With this, Noah's daughter walked out onto the ice! She walked up to a seal. She grabbed on to its flipper. Both the seal and Noah's daughter slipped through the ice and disappeared. "Get my daughter back!" Noah cried.

With this, Noah's son climbed down from the ark, walked up to a seal, grabbed on to its flipper. Both the seal and Noah's son disappeared under the ice. "Get my son back!" Noah cried out.

With this, Noah's wife walked up to a seal. She grabbed its flipper. Both the seal and Noah's wife disappeared through the breathing-hole. "Get my wife back!" Noah shouted.

"They won't be back until ice-break-up," a man said. "Go on, go on, grab a seal flipper and go after them!"

"No—no," said this Noah.

With this, the villagers went out onto the ice to hunt seals. People at home in the village were hungry. They caught many seals. On their way home, they shouted up, "Noah—come with us. We'll feed you until the ice-break-up. Just give us a few planks of wood."

"No," said Noah.

"Look—!" a man shouted. Everyone looked out onto the ice and saw Noah's wife curled up next to a breathing-hole. Farther on, Noah's son was curled up next to a breathing-hole. Farther on a little, Noah's daughter was curled up next to a breathing-hole. "They seem to be doing well," a man said.

"Wife! Daughter! Son!" Noah shouted loudly—it caused his wife, daughter, and son to startle and slip through the ice.

"How can I get them back?" Noah asked.

"Give the shaman your ark," a village man said.

"Go away," said this Noah.

The villagers kept Noah fed with scraps of food the rest of the winter. When the ice-break-up arrived, Noah's family did not get back on the ark. They chose to live with seals—or maybe the shaman chose that. You see what a shaman does—you don't always see the shaman!

Noah's ark was now floating again. But the ice had cracked open the bottom. The ark sank away into the sea. Noah was given a kayak and paddled it near to the village. "I don't like what happened here!" he said.

"Tell us what happened," a woman shouted out.

"A shaman made my family live with seals. A shaman took the animals from my ark. My ark sank away into the sea."

"The shaman didn't stab a broom into you," the woman said. "Stop complaining. Seals have good lives—be happy for your wife, daughter, son. They know how to get through winter."

Then Noah paddled in the southerly direction until nobody could see him.

Part II

A HELEN MISCELLANY

PRAYERS

Sometimes I would lie on Helen's bed reading while she sat at her desk, translating, composing a letter to one of her friends in linguistics all over the world, part of her obviously prodigious epistolary life. I noted addresses in Denmark, Japan, Canada, England. She once said to me, "I write at least one letter every day."

She preferred notebooks with either black or maroon covers. The maroon notebooks—at least those she had in Churchill—were reserved for linguistics, rough drafts of folktales, notations in Japanese, English, and Inuit phonetics. In the black notebooks, and ledgers, she kept a diary and archived her life as a bird-watcher. "I don't keep what people call a 'life list,'" she said. "To my mind that would reduce the joy of seeing birds to arithmetic. I've been with people who keep such lists. I consider it a kind of bragging. It's just my opinion, is all."

"You keep very exact records, though," I said.

"For my own memory, no one else's," Helen said. "I only took the one zoology course in university. A general sort of course."

"You always carry so many field guides with you?"

"Just about always."

"You have a—what is it—a Dutch-language field guide. Do you read Dutch, too?"

"I like the illustrations in that book. In particular, in that book."

In neat columns Helen wrote the names of birds she saw, geographical locales, time of day sighted, and so on. "I'm an autodidact of ornithology," she said. "Mostly self-taught—. When you're self-taught, of course, you're your own best *and* worst teacher. But that can't be helped, can it?"

"I thought you told me you had some formal classes at some point, in ornithology, Helen. It was—am I remembering this right?—out west in Canada. British Columbia, wasn't it?"

"Well, I'd call those *informal*, uh, lessons. Not classes, really. Not in a classroom situation."

"Oh."

"Yes, and it was complicated by—"

"By?"

"Romance."

"Complicated by romance."

"Yes. Complicated by romance. But still, I did learn quite a bit."

"I would imagine."

"—about birds. It was very, very useful knowledge. Knowledge gained, about birds out there, you see."

Helen also kept a separate black notebook for prayers. She let me read it on any number of occasions. Come to think of it, she was less guarded about this notebook than the ones having to do with linguistics or birds, ironically enough. "Prayers" was Helen's word for these compositions.

I remember that exactly. They were written in Japanese; she translated quite a few for me, upon request, and I requested that at least a dozen times while we were in Churchill and a few times in our subsequent correspondences between Japan and Canada.

To the best of my knowledge—she and I never discussed this—Helen's prayers did not echo any one religious sensibility. However, they all shared one thing in common: each was a request to see a bird. They each were a request to add, then, to Helen's "life list," no matter how she thought of it. In effect, these prayers to see birds elevated bird-watching to a spiritual plane, no doubt about that. Some were stated directly:

> I would like to see
> a red phalarope.

Or—and it made me laugh out loud when Helen translated this variation:

> I would like to see
> a red phalarope
> (please).

To my mind Helen's prayers did not betray outsized emotions, nor were they necessarily philosophical, except for the general and obvious idea that a prayer would be useless were there not some sort of powerful entity—perhaps God—who might be listening, or persuaded through elegant diction to listen, and thus be petitioned. Prayers, of course, are of the utmost intimate language (intimate dialogue), yet Helen's were never confessional. For instance, nowhere in her prayers, even the longer ones of ten or twelve lines, say, was her illness mentioned. The word "cancer" was never used. There was no reference or allusion to physical pain at all. My guess—and it is only a guess—is that Helen did not wish to use sympathy to barter with God. Had she even obliquely exploited her "medical condition," it would have been undignified, demeaning, because it would imply a belief in a hierarchy of suffering—therefore, those in the most pain, or those about to die, might exact first priorities of mercy. How could any feeling and thinking person at all alert to the human condition possibly be convinced of something as absurd as that?

Helen's prayers were never precisely haiku, nor did they, again as far as I knew, follow any compositional tradition. As I have said, for the most part they were rather declarative; all evidence of desire was monotonal. Her prayers had a utilitarian demeanor about them. Yet in the strictest sense, they were autobiographical, too, and in their own way revelatory as somewhat restrained entries in a diary:

I lost out as a Buddhist, worse as a Christian.
Never mind; I ask, please, to see a harlequin duck.
It would best be quite soon.★

I have in my possession all 116 of Helen's prayers to see birds; some she translated, some were translated, albeit

★This last line, naturally, evokes a sense of urgency without source.

roughly, by a graduate student at the University of Michigan a few years after Helen's death. Helen sent me the Japanese-language manuscript from Kyoto. It was typed on onionskin paper, which was what everyone used to type on. Each prayer has the title "Prayer One," "Prayer Two," and so on. The entire manuscript is titled "Prayers to See Birds," practical enough, and I say "manuscript" because why else title it if you don't see it to some extent as a work of literature? On the last page (in English and Japanese) is the sentence *Typed by Remington Typewriter in Kyoto, Japan, July 6, 1978*. Thirty-one days later Helen died in her brother and sister-in-law's house in Kyoto. I like thinking of Helen alert and strong enough to type up those pages, no matter over what length of time.

Later I wrote to Helen's brother and sister-in-law asking if the "Remington typewriter" referred solely to the one typed sentence in English on the last page of the manuscript. Arthur, Helen's brother, wrote back saying that, yes, it did, because her Japanese typewriter was made by a different company. "I know that you and Helen spoke often about typewriters," Arthur wrote in that same letter. "Helen told me as much. I suppose that last sentence of her manuscript was meant for your special bemusement."

In fact, a year or a little over a year after Helen passed away I wrote to Arthur offering to buy Helen's Remington typewriter. I suddenly wanted it. It was a bout of acquisition fever, I suppose, and I am not pleased to be the person who asked for the typewriter, but I did. There was greed resident in my nostalgia. I wanted to own an object connected to my and Helen's friendship. I do not know all that went into my

comporting myself so crudely; I cannot forgive myself for
it. It was Susanne, Helen's sister-in-law, who wrote back, a
prompt one-paragraph reply which ended by saying, "As for
Helen's English typewriter, you might recognize the font on
the very page you are now reading. Yes, Mr. Norman, I am
afraid that Arthur and I wish to keep the typewriter. You'll
understand. We use it, actually." When I read her letter I re-
called that Helen said of Susanne that she had about her "an
elegant restraint."

"I think I'd like to die quickly—I mean, at the very last,"
Helen had said. "I wouldn't want to be too aware of the
moment." It was about a week before we left Churchill. We
were having dinner. Arctic char, potatoes, thawed green
beans, as usual. "I mean, I don't want to have to have all
those tubes and such, in a cold hospital room."

"That's just not going to happen. Not from what you've
told me about your family in Japan."

"No, I suppose not. I shouldn't be speaking of this. Two
months knowing you, Howard Norman, I am speaking like
this. Quite unfair, actually. You know what, though? I
should do what this old woman I knew in Greenland did. I
really should."

"Which was?"

"About five or six years ago, I stayed in Greenland all
winter. I was taking life histories, and I was working with
one very old woman. She had cancer. There was no question as to what it was. A visiting doctor—maybe from the
World Health Organization or some such. There was a diag-
nosis. Well, one night, she went around and said good-bye,

she went right outside and disappeared. How cold—who knows, maybe minus fifty Fahrenheit, colder, probably. Out she went. All alone out she went, you know? Walked as far as strength allowed, I suppose, drank a bottle of whiskey top to bottom as my father used to say, lay down—perhaps. Perhaps took her clothes off to hurry it along. How cold out. You'd get numb to feeling quite quickly, right? Anyone knows that. There's a lot of good sense to what she did. I should pay attention to that. I didn't witness it for nothing—"

"Was that the last anyone saw of her?"

"It wasn't spoken about."

NOAH GOES ON A SEAL HUNT

This happened, this happened, and three people from away died, because a big wooden boat floated into Hudson Bay. It floated out on the horizon. The whole village saw it.

There was a rough wind. Gulls-blown-around wind. It was a rainy wind. Rain became snow.

"Look—out there!" a man said. "It's some kind of boat!"

"Let's go out to it," another villager said.

"Yes"—and it was agreed.

Some village men, women, children, a few dogs, all paddled out to the wooden boat. On the deck of this boat stood a man. Next to him stood his wife, his son, his daughter. Behind them stood animals such as the villagers had never seen. Strange-looking animals—one villager said, "I wonder how they might taste!"

"Hey, what's this boat?" a man called out.

"It is called an ark," the man on the deck shouted.

"What is your name?" another villager shouted up.

"Noah."

The villagers moved the sound of this name—Noah—around in their mouths. Noah, Noah, Noah, Noah.

"Noah," a village man said, "look out to the horizon. What do you see? It's something you should learn about—quickly!"

"I'm looking," said Noah. "But all I see is the horizon."

"Look more closely."

"I see the horizon, that's all," Noah said.

"Squint your eyes."

Noah squinted his eyes and looked far into the distance. "Still—nothing," he said.

"You see it," a villager said, "you just don't know what you are looking at. That's because you are not smart about things up here where we live. In this place. You are ignorant about things here. Maybe you're smart about things where you come from, but not here!"

"Tell me, then, what's out there?" Noah said.

"It's winter. You are looking at winter, gathering. It is heading this way. It is moving in fast. Look—there—see those gulls getting wind-tossed? Blown around—blown around. Watch out!"

Just then a seal flew in and landed next to Noah. It was now dead. "Look—the wind hunted a seal for you," a villager said. "Go ahead and cut it up and give some to your family. There's good seal oil, too."

"No—I don't know how to eat this seal," said Noah.

"Try the flippers, try the oil—don't eat the nose or whiskers," a village man shouted.

This made the villagers laugh.

"I don't want to eat a seal," said Noah.

"We're hungry, though," Noah's wife said. "We're hungry," his daughter said. "We're hungry, though," his son said.

"We still have some food," Noah said. "Some of our kind of food. Eat some of that."

"Roll that seal off your boat, then," a villager said. "Let us have it. We've never seen the wind hunt a seal like that before—it's luck. It's luck! Let us have it!"

"No," said Noah, and he rolled the seal off the other side of the ark and it sank away before any villagers could get to it.

"A man travels a long distance just to turn down a gift from the wind—a wind-hunted seal, the first one I've seen in my life!" said an old village man. "This Noah is unusual."

"Let's paddle away from this unusual man," another villager said.

"Yes"—and it was agreed. They paddled back to the village.

Winter arrived, seals gripped the ice near their breathing-holes. Noah saw polar bears hunting seals—Noah saw villagers hunting seals. Ice was all around the ark. During a blizzard the villagers didn't visit the ark, but when the weather cleared, they visited.

"Hey—Noah!" a village man shouted. "How many of your animals have you eaten?"

"I can't eat them," Noah said. "When we're done floating around, we're going back to where we came from. Then I'll let the animals go. I promised my God—he runs things. I promised I'd let the animals go."

The villagers on the ice fell to laughing. The sound of their laughter echoed out over the ice, and seals slipped through their breathing-holes, back into the water. "There's other spirits running things up here!" a village man shouted. "Ha, ha, ha!"

"Look—there!" another village man said. Everyone turned to look, and there, out on the ice, a black-and-white-striped horse was running. It did not know how to run on ice. It fell and slid, got up, fell, slid—then it fell through the ice.

"Now it's lost," a villager said. "It would've been better to have eaten it."

"I wonder how it tastes," said Noah's wife.

"I wonder how it tastes," said Noah's daughter.

"There's another one on the ark, here," said the son. "I'm going to kill it and cook it."

With this, Noah said, "No!"

"I wonder how it tastes," Noah's son said.

"Give us a few animals," a villager said. "Give us a few planks of wood from your ark. In return, we'll hunt and fish for you, and you will make it through winter. You can even live in our village with us—all winter, all winter. When the ice thaws and breaks up, we'll paddle you out to your ark, though the ice might crack it before then."

"No," said Noah.

"Why not go on a seal hunt with us, then?" a man said. "We'll take you along. What you learn you can use to help feed your family."

Noah went to the bottom of the ark, then he stepped out onto the ice. He fell a few times, then got his footing—much laughter. "Here's a sealskin parka," a woman said. Noah put it on.

Then they told Noah how to hunt a seal—quiet—crawl forward, don't speak loudly—they told him some things, they said, "You stand back, we'll go on ahead." They gave Noah a spear.

Soon they saw a seal up ahead—it was facing away from the

hunters, and the wind was blowing toward them—all for the good. "Now, stay back," a hunter whispered to Noah—but this hunter saw that on Noah's face was hunger and sadness, Noah had gone crazy in his head—Noah dropped to his knees and started to crawl toward the seal. "Stay back—stay back"—but Noah crawled toward the seal.

"At least don't stand up," a hunter said. But Noah stood up and the seal slid into the water.

Noah looked over at the ark. He saw his wife, daughter, and son crawling over the ice. They had been crawling in a proper manner toward the seal. As he watched, this happened: his wife, son, and daughter fell through the ice. This happened, this happened, and his family disappeared.

Now Noah was crazed by grief, sadness, and confusion—he had hunted a seal wrongly, he had seen his family sink away—so, now, he walked to the seal breathing-hole and tried to climb down through it!

The hunters hurried out to Noah, knocked him down, and dragged him across the ice back to the village. He had ice burns on his face. When they dragged him into the village, a woman said, "What happened to him?"

A man said, "He saw his family drop through the ice."

The villagers tied Noah up for days, to keep him from crawling out over the ice. In the meantime, they fed him bits of fish and seal, and kept him warm by seal-oil lamp. They took care of him; he howled often—He wept and said things that made no sense.

Everyone saw many animals from the ark walk out over the ice; they saw brightly colored birds fly away from the ark. "I wonder how those birds taste?" a few villagers said.

During the ice-break-up the ark sank. Noah was sent walking in the southerly direction—but when he got a ways from the village, he dropped to his knees and started to crawl. Nobody followed, they left him alone. "How far does he have to travel?" a village boy asked.

"I don't know," an old woman in the village said.

Later, some planks of wood from the ark rolled onto shore. The villagers set them out to dry. Later, when some villagers sat by the ark-wood fire, one said, "Noah might've killed his first seal, if only he hadn't stood up." They talked about that awhile.

TREATISE ON CHOKING

By the time I entered Helen's life and vice versa, she had for five years been working on her treatise, "Incidents of Choking in Inuit Folktales." She kept separate notebooks for this writing.

The central paradox of the treatise as a whole was that within the vast arctic landscape, which, as ship's captain Alfred Rohrem McCally said in 1890, "seems to have more air to breathe than any place on earth," many Inuit folktales depict people choking to death or frightfully close to it, either as the result of a shaman's malevolent reprisal or out of some sort of tremendous anxiety, or during a fight with a spirit who uses choking as a strategy of attack.

"I think I started noticing this first in Greenland," Helen told me. "I was having some respiratory problems of my own—so I might've been naturally preoccupied and drawn especially to such motifs, but who can say, really? Anyway, I started to ask about stories in which people choked, and started to think about the subject, and then about three years ago really began to work on this thing. I'll never finish it, of course, and in a way it's too academic for my tastes. Just another way to type up the arctic, isn't it?"

"Your chapter titles are—I guess I'd call them melodramatic."

"It went down the wrong pipe," Helen said.

"What?"

"I'm sure you've heard someone say that, at the dinner table, or in a restaurant. You know, when a person starts to cough and taps their chest, and has a slight worried look on their face? You know exactly what I'm talking about."

"Sure."

"What I'm saying is, that's a fairly dramatic moment, and what I started to notice in folktales was that it was described—choking—as happening to a person both alone and out in nowheresville—I've always loved that word. I heard it in London. I was eavesdropping on some kids, musicians, I think, and one looked around, bored, and said, 'This place is nowheresville.' Boy, was I pleased to hear that—So, anyway, I was collecting stories where some man would be standing out in the middle of nowheresville and begin choking. Or he'd be standing among a lot of people choking in public. Some shaman or other showing off his wares—a very nasty scene. 'Take that!'" Helen, sitting on her bed, thrust out her arm as if it was a fencing foil.

"Kind of a morbid subject, huh?"

"Breathtaking subject, actually."

"I give that a D minus, Helen."

"Deservedly so."

We were just sitting around, shooting the breeze as usual. While she was writing a letter, I was looking through her notebook. Some of the chapter titles were "Gasping for Air," "Bird Bones in Windpipe," "Blacking Out," "I Need Some

Air," "Dizziness—or, Feeling Dizzy." Each title was in reference to a specific incident in a folktale discussed in an ongo-
ing chapter in the treatise, but also it was apparent that
Helen was in a way collecting American slang, phrases that
delighted her—like "nowheresville." Captions of life.

"You think it's strange, my interest in these choking stories?"

"A whole treatise, Helen, that's dedicated."

"There are a lot of stories to be dedicated to."

"How many choking stories are you writing about, for
instance?"

"Oh, I'd say thirty or so."

"Somebody gets choked in each story?"

"Yes, but I didn't hear very many stories in which someone actually died. A few."

"Why do you think?"

"Because choking is *persuasive*. Like in that Noah story of
Mark's, when Noah starts choking on a piece of blubber and
the only word he can manage to speak is 'Yes.' That way he
agrees to everything he's asked!"

"Are you adding that story to your treatise?"

"Of course. Why not?"

"I'm having a lot of difficulty translating that story. But
now that you mention it, when Noah is choking, it's both
terrifying and funny at the same time!"

"The villagers want some of those animals and some
wood, and he won't, as usual, give them anything, so they
make him choke and he says, 'Yes—yes—yes—yes,' and so
he has to then give them some wood."

"I'm having a lot of trouble getting that story right."

"Boo hoo."

"What do you mean, 'choking is persuasive'?"

"Whoever is causing a person to choke usually gets his way."

"As simple as that?"

"As simple as that."

One evening—Helen had gone to sleep at about 8 p.m.—I read a section of the treatise more carefully than I previously had; her notes, her impressions, her folkloric anecdotes, extended disquisitions and queries, all were fascinating. And of course it's a gift to be able to read what a person has been working on for so long, anyway. On the bed Helen was breathing easily, and I hoped she was a world away from pain. To this day I recall a passage in her treatise from a story she had translated into both English and—on the facing page—Japanese. (Reading it, I realized that Helen could most definitely have translated Mark's Noah stories more deftly—and accurately—into English than I could, let alone into Japanese. Probably into French, too!) It was a piece of dialogue between a devious shaman and an Inuit hunter who had become his adversary:

"I've just stuck a guillemot in your throat," said the shaman. "Now, give me all of your best sled dogs!"

With this, the man opened his mouth to speak, but only the voice of a guillemot came out, "O-waahk O-waahk—" squalling voice of a guillemot!

The shaman, who could understand the language of guillemots, said, "You have made a good decision."

He took all the dogs and flew with them out to the horizon. Then the guillemot flew out of the man's throat and the man took a lot of deep breaths. He was worn out. He went to sleep—right there, on the ground, he slept. As he slept he took deep breaths. When he woke he took deep breaths.

As I was reading along Helen woke and said, "Not reading my diary, I hope."

"I was just waiting for you to wake up so we could listen to the radio a while," I said.

"Because if you read my personal diary, I'll ask Mark Nuqac if he knows somebody to put a curse on you, and bad things will befall you."

"Tea?"

LAUREL AND HARDY

The motel office had a television, and on a few nights Helen and I watched. On one of those nights, Mark and his ten-year-old grandson joined us, along with Mark's half sister, if I got the family configuration right. Also present were a few other children. Everyone ate chocolate bars during the Laurel and Hardy movie, I have forgotten the title. Mark's half sister's name was Sarah, and while everyone else was talking all through the movie, she remained absolutely silent, while Thomas, the grandson, translated now and then whatever Laurel or Hardy was saying on-screen. The only words he didn't have to translate for her were "Stan" and "Ollie." The plot took place in medieval times. Laurel and Hardy were dressed in ridiculous, frilly costumes. At one point, Ollie falls into a pond and Stan paces the bank, anxiously vigilant, waiting for his pal to pop up for air. More time passes than any man, even Houdini, could possibly stay underwater holding his breath. Stan now is quite agitated in his face-scrunched-up, inimitably comic and heart-wrenching way. Still, Ollie has not surfaced—he does not come up, he does not come up—until finally Stan squeaks the wonderful line, "Ollie, oh Ollie, come up, you'll catch a cold!"

I understood then from Sarah's Inuit that she had asked
Thomas what Stan was so worried about, and instead of
translating, Thomas faked a sneeze. Sarah caught the absurd-
ity and laughed very hard.

HIS MAJESTY'S SHIP *ROSAMOND*

Helen had read extensively in the ethnography, linguistics, and history of the Hudson Bay region—in Japanese, French, English—whereas I had lacked industry. I quote my zoology professor, Arvin Williams, who said, "You don't lack know-how or IQ, you lack industry." When I saw Helen's arctic bibliography listed in one of her notebooks, I could only manage a feeble understatement, "You really did your homework, didn't you?" though of course, considering her years in the arctic, she was far beyond being a student.

How *had* I prepared? Only by reading a few nineteenth-century explorers' journals, a few ethnographic monographs (I had one on Inuit kayaks with me in Churchill), and a general history of northern expansion. I had listened to several "instructional" tapes in Inuit, to at least apprentice myself to the sound of the language, if little else. And I'd worked with an Inuit speaker, Mrs. Roy Barnes, the wife of a school-teacher, in Toronto; Mrs. Barnes was an Inuit woman, age fifty-four, who had been born in Rankin Inlet but partly raised in several Caribou Inuit communities. I met with Mrs. Barnes for five hours four days a week for three weeks at my apartment on Ulster Street in Toronto, during which time she did not speak English at all. She always brought cookies or carrot cake. She had constructed actual lessons, stuck assiduously to her lesson plans, the result of which was that I gained a basic Inuit vocabulary and perhaps tentative confidence in my potential ability to speak it. But after our last lesson, as we shared cookies and coffee, when Mrs. Barnes smiled and said, "You have a good ear for this language," it seemed less a compliment, or encouragement, than what was left below the line in an old-fashioned vertical arithmetic: subtract all that I wasn't or perhaps would never be, what remained was that I "heard" with some accuracy. "You shouldn't expect too much from just three weeks."

Hidden in this kind advice, I felt, was a forecast of linguistic doom.

"Plainly stated," Helen said, "it's a very, very difficult language."

As for my lack of intellectual preparation, Helen did not mince words. "Unprofessional, really," she said, wagging a finger like a schoolmarm. On the other hand, it was instructive and even solacing when Helen acknowledged that the actual experiences one has in a place to a great extent displace research. "I've noticed this time and again," she said. "No matter how much you read, no matter how many people you talk to in advance, so much flies out the window within a few hours. I'm not suggesting you don't consider research part of being a good linguist, or translator. I'm only saying that the minute you step off the airplane much of it— what's the right American phrase?—takes a backseat. For instance, you can read every study in existence about polar bears, but when you first see one—"

"I feel pretty stupid, though, not reading 'every study in existence.'"

"Look at it this way," Helen said, laughing a little, "no research—no preconceptions. Blank mind, good mind—as Buddhists might say, or something close to that."

Given the vast discrepancy, however, between Helen's and my "book knowledge," as she put it, I was absolutely thrilled to discover that indeed we did have one book in common. When I saw it on her desk I said, no doubt with unbridled glee, "Hey, I own that! I've read that!"

"Oh, I've read it any number of times," Helen said. "It's remarkable, isn't it?"

The book was *Narrative of a Voyage to Hudson's Bay in His Majesty's Ship* Rosamond (subtitled on the cover, *containing some account of THE NORTH-EASTERN COAST OF AMERICA AND THE TRIBES INHABITING THAT REMOTE REGION*), written by Lieutenant Edward Chappell, R.N., and published in London in 1817.

"Where did you find it?" Helen said.

"In a used-book store in Toronto. In a stack of things. You?"

"Less, uh, accidentally."

"I like the written language, the sound of it, you know. It reads like a novel."

"That was the language of the time it was written in. Educated, formal, somewhat—what? Florid."

"You mean—?"

"I mean, even a very ignorant, even a bigoted observation can be obfuscated—hidden a bit—because of the *flair* of the writing. Some terrible stupidities in these old journals, condescensions, toward *Esquimaux*—you know, the French derivation. The sound of the language, the style, is all intimate and full of astonishment in some of those journals. Part of it might've been historical naïveté, but part, I think, tries to convince a king or someone, a reader, of the superiority of the writer's culture. France or England, et cetera. My literature professor said style is suspect; you want it to serve clarity, to serve actual intent."

"I'm a bit over my head with that, Helen."

"All I'm referring to is: the old explorers' journals are sometimes written by men of great vision and sympathy and understanding, but sometimes there's an arrogance and narrow, belligerent philosophy that doesn't allow for actual experience—you know, what is right there in front of you—to have any effect whatsoever."

"Did you find this true of Chappell?"

"Not usually, no. And his report is full of wonderful descriptions and events. And some lovely passages; you could almost recite them like a poem."

I picked up her copy and read from a middle page at whim, which, ironically, had to do with Churchill: "'Whilst we were at *York Fort*, we received information that the factory at *Churchill* had been burnt to the ground, in the month of *November*, 1813. The miseries which the people of that place suffered during the remainder of the winter were very great. As there were seventy-three chests of gunpowder in the warehouse at the time the conflagration took place, their whole attention was occupied in removing away the powder to prevent an explosion; and by the most strenuous exertions they succeeded in this undertaking; but the time lost prevented their being able to save a mouthful of provisions, or a single utensil, from the flames. An old outhouse that had escaped destruction, and a few tents which they erected of reindeer skins, served them as habitations during the remainder of the winter; and, as if Providence had taken especial care to provide for their necessities, partridges abounded to a greater degree than had been known for many years before. Of course, these birds proved a seasonable supply to the sufferers; particularly as the partridges are so very tame, that they suffer themselves to be driven into nets, by which means large quantities are taken at one time.

" 'A family in England would be justly esteemed objects of great pity, if they were burnt out of their home in the midst of winter, although many friendly habitations might be humanely open for their reception. What then, comparatively speaking, must have been the situation of the *Churchill* people—driven out by the flames in the middle of a *November* night, on the shores of a frozen ocean, with the thermometer meter 78 degrees below the freezing point, without any shelter save that of a decayed outhouse, no bedding, no cooking utensils, no immediate nourishment, and no final prospect of relief, except from a reliance on the adventitious aid of their fowling-pieces! Such a night must surely be allowed to have had its share of horrors. But heroic strength of mind is the characteristic of the *European* traders to *Hudson's Bay*; and this alone enabled the people of *Churchill* to escape all the evils attendant on such a calamity.' "

Helen nodded and said, "I wonder if those 'people of Churchill' asked the *Esquimaux* for help."

"There seems to have been a lot of wood to trade for help, huh?"

"Not if Noah was mayor of Churchill. Isn't that what the head of a town, or town council, was called, 'mayor'?"

"It might have been magistrate, I don't know. It could have been mayor."

"I wonder if the memory of that explosion got handed down to Mark Nuqac's generation."

"Why don't you read him that section of Chappell's report, Helen?"

"I just might."

"Tell me his reaction if you do, okay?"

Helen took the book from me, paged through it, and found the passage she was looking for. "You just reminded me of something Lieutenant Chappell wrote—listen to this; it's where some native people have got aboard the *Rosamond*: 'On board the ship, they were exceedingly curious in viewing everything: but however astonished or delighted they might appear in the first sight of any novelty, yet ten minutes was the utmost limit of their admiration. The pigs, cats, and fowls, attracted their attention in so remarkable a manner, as to indicate a certainty of their not having seen any such animal before.'"

"That sounds familiar!"

Helen improvised, "The giraffes, hippopotamus, gazelles, and lions attracted their attention . . ."

"Yep, it's important to see it from both points of view.

The Esquimaux's *and* Noah's. I mean, in order to maybe understand the stories better."

Helen again read: " 'Shortly afterwards, we imagined that we could distinguish the sound of voices through the fog; we immediately beat the drum, to point out our situation; and, in a few minutes, we plainly heard the shouting of the *Esquimaux*: they soon came alongside the ship, with the usual expressions of delight. It is really surprising that this people should venture so far from the land, in such frail barks, through a mass of ice which is enough to daunt a *European*, even in a stout-built ship.' "

"That passage could apply to one of Mark's stories," Helen said.

Toward the end of our stay in Churchill there was a particular evening and night on which Helen fell into a near-stupor of pain that seemed bereft even of the humor Helen could mine from her own despondency. I felt a definite panic that the cancer her physicians predicted would give her more time—months, in fact, if not a full year—had opted for murder *now*. Her groans, paleness, and grimaces scared me. It felt like an invisible murderer had entered the room.

"Helen, I think we should get you to a hospital, right now," I said.

"I'm not doing what you think I might be doing."

"You look pale, Helen. Your hands feel clammy."

"I've been pale and clammy, as you say, ten thousand times. I ache deeply inside, and I'm having stupid, bad thoughts. Mark would say, 'Spirits are using her.' Maybe they are." She dozed off for a moment, opened her eyes, and said, "Would you consider reading Lieutenant Chappell's report to me?"

"Of course. Yes."

"Just until I nod off. I like that phrase, 'nod off.'"

This was about eight o'clock or eight-thirty at night. I began to read from the preface, which, in Chappell's day, was called the *Advertisement*: "'Towards the close of the year 1814, a young naval officer, Lieutenant *Chappell*, of His Majesty's ship *Rosamond*, who had recently returned, for the second time, from an expedition to the *North-eastern* coast of *America*, brought to *Cambridge* a collection of the dresses, weapons, &c. of the *Indians* inhabiting *Hudson's Bay*; requesting that I would represent these curiosities to the Public Library of the University.'"

The notion that Helen's exhaustion and medications, in concert with being read to, would act as a soporific proved false—or, as Lieutenant Chappell wrote, a *falsehood of some note*—because Helen stayed awake through my reading of the *entirety* of Chappell's report, *Advertisement* all the way to page 246, where he ends the narrative proper by writing: "I shall here conclude this Narrative; merely adding, that the *Rosamond* and her convoy again sailed from the *Orkneys* on the 7th of *November*, and arrived safe at the *Nore* on the 17th of the same month; when an inspection having been made of the *Rosamond*'s defects, she was reported to be totally unfit for sea, in consequence of the damage she had sustained amongst the ice of *Hudson's Straits*; and she was accordingly put out of commission, and immediately advertised to be sold out of His Majesty's service."

(I did not read the Appendixes: "Statement of the Variation of the Compass," "Table of the Voyages of the Company Ships, since the year 1773," "Thermometrical Observations," "Dresses, &c. OF THE ESQUIMAUX INDIANS in Hudson's Strait, "A Vocabulary of the LANGUAGE of the CREE or KNISTENEAUX INDIANS," though the language in those was decidedly evocative.)

It was now about 2 or 3 a.m., I think, though more likely I had lost track of time, which is the best way to read, or listen to someone read. "Thank you, Howard Norman," Helen said when I set the book down on the bedside table. "You're second only to the CBC announcers. Of course, *they're* not available upon request, are they."

SEAL HUNTERS LIVE ON THE ARK AWHILE

A big wooden boat appeared on the horizon. Some village men paddled out to it in kayaks. When they got to the boat, they heard, "Two of you can stay—the rest of you go away!" The villagers saw a long wooden stick with bristles waving in the air and ravens flying off the bristles. The ravens landed on another part of the boat.

"I've seen that tool before," a man said. "I saw it in a dream."

"Let's find out who's sweeping ravens," another man said.

"Yes, it's not right to invite two to stay and tell the rest of us to leave," another man said. "Very selfish."

A few men climbed up the side of the boat. While they were climbing, winter arrived. Sometimes this happens, winter lands suddenly as a raven. Now it was winter.

The men stood on the deck of the boat. Then they saw a European man dressed in a white coat, but it wasn't made of sealskin. "Hey—was that you shouting? Was that you sweeping ravens away?" a man said.

"Yes—get off my ark," the man in the white coat said.

"Is that what this boat is called?"

"Yes."

"What's your name?" a villager said.

"Noah."

"Noah," the villager said, "you can't blame ravens for coming around. That's what they do. Ravens are curious. Every time a person paddles out in a kayak, ravens come by to see if a fish is being caught or cleaned. They like the fish guts, for one thing. They'll squabble right on a kayak, if fish guts are seen. Gulls, too. They beg for food. Hey, hey—what's that smell?"

"I have a lot of animals below deck," this Noah said.

"Noah, what kind of animals, Noah?" a villager asked. "Seals, white bear, ptarmigan?"

"I don't know those," said Noah. "I don't have those with me."

"Where is your family?"

"They died."

"Did any of the animals kill them?"

"No."

"How did it happen, then?"

"One by one, they jumped from the ark and drowned."

"Come to our village, tell everyone what happened. We'll find you a new wife. It's winter now. You'll starve out here."

"Go away. I'm staying on the ark."

"Well, can you eat the animals below deck?"

"I won't. Go away!"

"Noah-no-family says go away," a villager said. "All right, we're off to hunt seals, then."

When they arrived at the seal grounds, they spread out and leaned over seal breathing-holes. Soon many ravens arrived. "We're curious about the ark," a raven said. "We're all flying over to it."

"Watch for Noah's broom, it's got sharp bristles," a man said.

"We heard about it," a raven said.

The ravens flew to the ark. A villager said, "Let's hunt seals a few more days. Then we'll go to the ark."

They caught seals, lashed them to their sleds, then went to the ark. When they got there they saw ravens swirling about. Some had broom bristles in their beaks. "Hey—hey—Noah!" a hunter shouted.

"Get these birds out of here!" Noah cried. "I know you sent them!"

"We told you ravens are curious."

"Get them away from me!"

"Give us some planks of wood, we'll chase off the ravens," a man said.

"All right," said Noah.

He pried off some planks. He dropped them to the ice. The hunters spoke to the ravens. Most of them flew off. "We know what it's like having too many visitors," a hunter called up to Noah. "One time all of my cousins stayed the winter, my wife's cousins, too. But we took them in. It was winter. They were hungry."

With this, the hunters climbed up onto the ark. They started living there. They ate what animals they found on the ark. They liked the taste of some; they hated the taste of others. "This is good—this isn't!" "This isn't a bad place to live awhile," one man said. "Yes," another man said, "we can visit our families easily, then come back out here. There's unusual things to eat." They settled in for a long visit.

Finally, Noah said, "I'll give you many more planks, go away."

"No," said a hunter. "Stop complaining. We're not poking you with knives, we're not poking you with ice chisels, we're not making you get rid of our dogs' fleas. Stop complaining. Sit and eat a meal with us."

Many days went by.

Some colorful birds flew off, but otherwise the hunters ate most of the animals Noah had on the ark. There was much talk about this, how they tasted, what they looked like, what their voices were— "That one was unusual—that one was unusual." When the ice-break-up arrived, the hunters paddled kayaks back to their village. There were many holes in the ark where planks had been pried off. The ark sank away into the sea. But the hunters had left behind a kayak for Noah and he paddled it clumsily to shore. "You can stay here," a woman said.

"No, I'm leaving," said Noah.

"Do you know how to travel without an ark?" a man said.

"I can walk."

"You no longer have a family where you came from. Stay, we'll find you a new wife."

"I'll try and find one where I come from."

The villagers walked south with Noah a ways, then turned back—a few ravens kept going, too. They were curious. Noah never returned—nobody ever knew if he got home, either. That is what happened.

THE MAN WHO HELD TWO KNIVES

The Inuit Cultural Institute was in Eskimo Point, a community largely developed by whites, or Europeans, for administration and mining purposes and whose population in the late 1970s was growing rapidly. Eskimo Point, too, was justifiably famous for having amongst its citizens some of the most remarkable, prodigious, and skilled carvers and sculptors; work from Eskimo Point is in private collections and museums all over the world. Mark's nephew Thomas accompanied Helen one day up to Eskimo Point, where she purchased a narrative sculpture called *The Man Who Held Two Knives*.

When she returned the next day, I saw *The Man Who Held Two Knives* prominently displayed on her writing desk, among papers, books, and other paraphernalia of the basically makeshift situation of life in a motel. "There's a wonderful cooperative up there," Helen said. "I saw carvings in bone, ivory, antlers—lots of soapstone. But this one really knocked me out."

I picked up *The Man Who Held Two Knives*, not only to admire the craftsmanship but to feel its weight, its solidity, and observe its detail close-up. I referred to it as a "narrative sculpture" for two reasons. First, the sculptor, whose name was Lucy, had told the person who sold the work to Helen, "I dreamed what the man in the carving is doing." Of course a dream is a narrative; in this instance, however, the artist herself defined the autobiographical origin, "I dreamed . . ." but also, to some extent, takes responsibility for the action depicted in the sculpture *because* she had dreamed it.

"I don't know if Lucy believes that dreams enter a person," Helen said, "or if dreaming's a creative act all on one's own. I didn't talk with her. The salesman in the cooperative told me what Lucy said. I didn't hear it from Lucy herself."

The second reason I refer to the sculpture as "narrative" is that a folded-up written story had accompanied Helen's purchase. Therefore *The Man Who Held Two Knives* depicts a moment frozen in time, even though the work itself is kinetic, it has animation, a kind of life force. When you look at *The Man Who Held Two Knives*, you are entering the life of the figure in medias res.

He stands about ten inches high, made of gray, grainy soapstone. His head is almost perfectly round; his eyes are etched slants, his mouth askew, there is no nose. His upper body is a triangular mass, his legs thick and short, though each of his arms is of plausible human dimensions. His feet are not clearly defined as feet; it is more that the legs widen at the ground. His right arm is angled 45 degrees upward, his left arm is angled 45 degrees downward. There are no hands to speak of, but rather knives in place of hands, so that there is no question as to whether the knives (and violent action associated with knives) are a physical extension of the body. The figure is therefore not "holding" knives but is partly *composed* of knives—sculpturally, at least, symbolically, most definitely—no matter what Lucy had titled her work of art.

The sculpture is a forensic tableau. At the figure's left lies the head of a seal, whiskers included, and at the figure's right lies the head of an Inuit man whose expression is a fixed grimace with broken teeth. Oddly, he is wearing snow goggles.

A seal was hunted; a man was murdered.

In a monograph, *Eskimo Point/Arviat*, published in Winnipeg, ethnographic art historian Bernadette Driscoll writes, "In a curious way, the procurement of food is implicit in the very act of Eskimo Point carving. In recent interviews a number of the artists responded to the question 'Why do you carve?' with the statement 'To purchase the equipment and supplies I need to hunt,' or, more explicitly, 'To put food on the table.' A very basic equation, that: sell artwork to make money in order to make a living in the more traditional, ancient manner. A dignified way to comport oneself on the planet.

So, Lucy had dreamed of a man doing an ill deed within an altruistic context. Still, according to the written story that came with *The Man Who Held Two Knives*, this man had murdered *in order to* provide for his family, a stunning ethical complication.

A man went out to hunt seals. He had his scrapers and a long, sharp spear. He also had two knives. He went many days with no luck. Then he saw another man who had just killed a seal. He offered the man something for it. When the man said no, the other raised both of his knives and with one stabbed. That is what happened. That is what I saw.

"Lucy's dream has the quality of direct testimony—you know, as in a courtroom. Doesn't it?" Helen said.

"Yeah, like she's been brought in as the star witness."

"'Lucy, what did you see happen out there in nowheresville?'"

I set *The Man Who Held Two Knives* back on the table. "Why did this one catch your eye?"

"Oh, I don't know. I think partly it was knowing that a woman had made it. And partly, I suppose, because it's so striking; you just feel so much energy from it. And sadness, too. Strange, the whole scene it depicts, don't you think? I don't know. It's both grotesque and beautiful all at once. It's like hearing a story you wish you'd never heard, about something you wished never had happened. But of course it *did* happen and you *did* hear it."

"Yes, Helen, but it was just a dream."

"Think what you wish."

A USEFUL MELANCHOLY

Before I met Helen I had not heard of Ryunosuke Akutagawa. Then I saw the quote "What good is intelligence if you cannot discover a useful melancholy?" taped to her typewriter.

"He is my most beloved writer," she said. "He is my favorite writer."

In his introduction to the collection *Rashomon*, scholar-translator Howard Hibbett writes, "To sketch the background and temperament of Ryunosuke Akutagawa is to risk a melancholy cliché. He was brilliant, sensitive, cynical, neurotic; he lived in Tokyo, went to the University, taught briefly, and joined the literary staff of a newspaper. Even his early suicide [in 1927, at thirty-five] only heightens the portrait of a modern Japanese intellectual, the double victim of an unsympathetic society and a split culture. But it is a vague composite portrait. For Akutagawa himself, aloof, elusive, individual, remains withdrawn behind the polished façade of his collected works. All that needs to be known about the author, besides the name stamped on the binding, may be found within these poems, essays, miscellaneous writings, and more than a hundred beautifully finished stories."

Helen displayed a framed magazine or book jacket pho-

tograph of Akutagawa on her desk. Looking at the camera,
it's as if Akutagawa wants us to dismiss his youthful hand-
someness as a fraudulent representation of a tormented inner
life. With his intense sidelong glance of preoccupation—or
dismissal of earthly concerns—he seems to judge the sparse,
café-life tableau of table and teacup as an annoying
"writerly" cliché. Weary, sardonic smile, sensual mouth, di-
sheveled black hair combed back from a high forehead on a
long face, his is one of the most severely enigmatic expressions I have ever seen. I think it is safe to say that in the
West, Akutagawa is known best as the author of the collection of stories *Rashomon*; a story in that collection, "In a
Grove," which centers on the rape of a traveling wife in
front of her husband by a thuggish stranger, an incident re-
lated from seven points of view, including that of a ghost,
served as the basis for the famous film *Rashomon*, directed by
Akira Kurosawa and starring Toshiro Mifune.

When Helen translated the quote on her typewriter, I
said, "Where did Akutagawa write that?"

"In a letter, I think," Helen said. "Or an essay."

"And do you agree with it?"

"Well, it is a question, after all. It can't be completely answered. But you can think about it. You can enter into a
kind of philosophical dialogue with it, can't you? But finally,
yes, I do agree. Melancholy seems just the right mood to
keep a clear perspective on life. Yes. Yes, I do agree. What
do you think?"

If Helen were alive today I would be able to answer, "I
have thought about that question practically every day."
Which is the truth.

Helen loaned me *Rashomon* and another book in an English edition written by Akutagawa, *A Fool's Life*, whose fifty-one elegantly composed vignettes make for a kind of literary suicide note. It begins with a letter-dedication to a friend, Kume Masao; in part this reads, "I exist now in a most unhappy happiness. But strangely without remorse. Only that I feel sorry for those who had me as husband, father, son. Good-bye. In the manuscript, *consciously* at least, there is no attempt to justify myself."

After reading *A Fool's Life* and *Rashomon* the world—and I search for diction that allows ebullience—"opened up anew." I fairly begged Helen for a reading list in Japanese fiction, works in English translation, of course. On her list was Kawabata, Akutagawa, Soseki, Junichiro Tanizaki, Ibuse. "After that, you're on your own," she said. "But these will keep you for a good long while, I bet."

But over the weeks I did not leave that quote alone. Finally, I realized that I had a specific curiosity about it. I wondered to what extent the quote ("What good is intelligence if you cannot discover a useful melancholy?") vindicated Helen's previously existing melancholia—as she described her "normal" state of mind—or did her adoration for Akutagawa require her to adopt his epigrammatic philosophy. Of course, when I finally mustered up enough courage to ask her, my inquiry lacked, to say the very least, sophistication: "Helen, why's that quote so important to you? I mean, it's on your typewriter, so you read it every day, don't you."

"It's haunting, that's the thing," she said. "I can't entirely explain it. I won't try—but, well, you read that story 'In a Grove,' didn't you?"

"Yes. And I'd like to read it again before giving it back."

"Well, the ghost's testimony is from the afterlife, you re-member? The quote is like that, I suppose. My beloved Akutagawa is dead and gone. But—and I can only imagine how this might sound—he speaks to me."

NOAH AND THE FLOOD

One day just before winter arrived, some villagers saw a lot of sea-gulls swirling up from a big wooden boat. "Hey—look—let's go out and see why the gulls landed there! Let's go look at this boat close-up."

"Should we bring spears?" a man said.

"Yes," another man said.

The villagers paddled out in kayaks to the boat. When they got there, a man appeared on deck. "My name is Noah," this man said. "Go away!"

"What's this boat called?"

"It's called an ark—go away!" this Noah shouted down.

"Is your family with you?"

Three people stood next to Noah now—"This is my wife, my son, my daughter," Noah said. "Go away!"

"Why are you here?" a village man asked.

"Where we come from, there was a big flood," said Noah's wife. "We got on this ark and floated away in the rain."

"Who built this boat?" a man said.

"My husband," said Noah's wife.

"Why did you have to leave home?"

"People all around us were behaving badly—doing bad things.

Our strongest spirit—God—caused a flood and they drowned. Everybody drowned except us and all the animals on the ark."

"What kinds of animals?" a village man said.

With this, a lot of big animals—and colorful birds—appeared on the deck of the boat. "It's good we brought our spears," a village man said. "Push those animals into the water, we'll get them before they sink away—we'll catch some, kill them, and eat them."

"No," said Noah.

"What did people do, where you came from—what made this God so angry?" a man asked.

"They were greedy," said Noah. "They killed each other. They stole things from each other."

The villagers all were laughing hard—they laughed hard, and the laughing went on a long time. "In a village north of here," a man finally said, "somebody stabbed somebody else, but we didn't have a flood. In a village north of here, somebody took somebody else's wife—they ran off together. We didn't have a flood. In a village north of here, somebody hit somebody else on the head with a rock, he died. But we didn't have a flood." In a village north of here, a man reined up his dogs badly, the dogs got away and choked and died, but we didn't have a flood. In a village north of here, a woman poisoned her husband and ran off with the man who had provided the poison. No flood—no flood."

"Where we come from, there was a flood," Noah's wife said.

Soon winter arrived. The ark was stuck in the ice. "Noah," a man called up, "bring your family to our village. Give us a few animals, a few planks of wood, we'll get you through the winter. Otherwise, you'll starve."

"No," said this Noah.

"All right," a villager said, "but at least let your family come with us."

"All right," said Noah.

The villagers set out with Noah's family. But instead of going to their home village, they traveled to a village to the north. When they arrived, a man said, "Did you see that big wooden boat out to sea?"

"Yes," said a man in this new village.

"Noah—that's his name—is on the boat. This is his wife, his daughter, his son. We're leaving them with you for a while."

Now Noah's wife, son, and daughter were living in this new village. That very night, Noah's wife took out some pieces of food from an animal on the ark. A haunch and neck, from a strange animal. These new villagers weren't giving them anything to eat, so they ate this, from the ark. Right away this happened: Noah's wife ran off with a man from the village; but first, she knocked the man's wife out with a rock. Noah's son stabbed a man, then tried to run off with that man's wife, but the man knocked Noah's son down. Noah's son ran out and didn't return. Noah's daughter found her brother half dead on the ice a few days later. Soon after, Noah's daughter fed some sled dogs pieces of her clothes soaked in seal oil, the dogs choked and a few dogs died. The next morning, Noah's son and daughter were sent to the next village to the south—but there was no flood.

When the ice-break-up arrived, Noah's wife paddled a kayak back to the ark. "Where have you been?" asked Noah.

"I ran off with a man from a village to the north," she said, "but, finally, I choked him a little and ran off again, and now I'm here."

"What about our son, what about our daughter?"

Noah's wife told Noah all that had happened in that village to the north. "Oh—Oh—Oh" said Noah, weeping. "Oh-oh-oh."

In a few days the ark was floating free of ice, and Noah's son and daughter paddled out in kayaks. They all floated in the southerly direction. But the ice had cracked the hull planks wide open and the ark sank away. "Which village should we paddle to?" asked Noah's wife.

"Not the village to the north," said Noah's daughter.

The village to the south took them in. "What will you do now?" a man asked.

"We'll walk in the southerly direction," Noah said. "Yes," said Noah's daughter. "Yes," said Noah's son. "Yes," said Noah's wife. The next day, they did that. They never came back. They didn't come back to the village to the north—or the village to the south.

Part III

TO BECOME A BIRD OF
THE SEA AND CLIFFS

REINCARNATION

Now here was an unusual sentence: "I've decided to become a bird of the sea and cliffs."

Calendar-wise it is difficult to recall just when Helen first introduced the subject of reincarnation into our conversations. I think it may have been the first week of October, a little more than a month after our first meeting. However, once such a thing is mentioned, from that moment on it becomes a presence if not a preoccupation. It was for me, at least; *Helen is thinking about this.*

We had walked out to Cape Merry, the rocky promontory at the mouth of the Churchill River. From this point you can scan the river, look out at old Fort Prince of Wales, or out over Hudson Bay itself. The tides are wild, the waters of sea and river commingle turbulently and, especially in summer, there's an impressive exhibit of wildlife. In June, for instance, after the ice-break-up flotillas of ducks and loons drift in and out of the tides. Also, pods of seals and beluga whales arrive to feed on schools of the small fish called capelin. Squalling flocks of terns, gulls, and jaegers wheel above the whales and ride on icebergs and ice floes. The river and bay, as early-nineteenth-century naturalist Robert T. Capmore wrote, "constantly reconfigure their surface," breaking into jigsaw pieces of ice, one of the world's great floating sculpture gardens. In summer, when the sun sets around 10 or 10:30 p.m., it is an especially dramatic time to watch birds and whales at Cape Merry. (Since 1977 I have taken photographs at midnight or 1 a.m., though, at its darkest, the light is crepuscular.)

At 1 p.m. we had met, Helen and I, at the Churchill Hotel and set out walking with an Inuit man named George—I never learned his last name—driving a dilapidated dark green pickup behind us. Helen, it turned out, had arranged this, "in case I get too tired." George had a rifle in the front seat with him; one had to be alert for polar bears. Helen had paid George twenty dollars Canadian. He kept about thirty yards or so behind us. "Today—at least right now," Helen said, "I have an unusual amount of stamina and want to take the longest walk possible."

"Sounds good," I said.

"If you get eaten by a bear, who should I telephone with the news?"

"Come to think of it, nobody."

"That would simplify things."

Cape Merry is about three kilometers from Churchill proper. We walked northwest on Kelsey Boulevard—the main street—then out toward the grain elevators. At the outskirts of town we turned left over the railroad tracks, the wind picked up, and there was the slightest confetti of snow as we took the road to the area known as the Flats. The spare, makeshift houses and the poverty were striking, and could only be somewhat sentimentally dignified by a phrase such as explorer-bird-artist Mark Catesby used in the late 1700s to describe a seaboard shanty community, "perhaps a place where history hoards its cast-aways, houses its most terrible and beautiful secrets." We looked out over the stretching mudflats. Scarce few birds remained past late August or early September, but, happily, we caught a glimpse of a snow bunting plus lots of common ravens and herring gulls. In another moment we saw two dunlins, which surprised us, because we had read that dunlins were a rare sighting this late in the year. "I know how they feel," Helen said.

"What do you mean?"

"Well, everybody else has gone off, haven't they? But you just can't quite get yourself to leave."

"There's no reason you couldn't stretch your stay in Churchill another few weeks, is there?"

"That wasn't what I was talking about, really. But no matter."

Then we saw a group of five or six common eiders, perhaps slightly more likely to be seen in early October, though most eiders had already left. With each bird sighted Helen checked her watch, marked the time, and noted the place in a small notebook.

Gazing at the mudflats empty, for the most part, of birds, Helen quoted Tabuboku Shinoda, a thirteenth-century artist she was particularly fond of, who had lived in a small house by the sea:

I have been drawing shorebirds. Each evening when they fly off to their secret haunts for the night, I am not merely a little forlorn. The cries of the birds I have drawn echo in my heart, as though my heart was the beach itself.

George accidentally honked the truck's horn, a raspy blurt, which startled us. When we looked back he shrugged apologetically, his wide red-brown face, unkempt hair, exaggerated smile like a mischievous child's. "Just wanted you to know where I was, eh?" he shouted out the driver's-side window. Then he tapped the horn a moment, rusty erratic beeps.

Then, an unexpected confession. "How George just honked the horn like that," Helen said. "It sounded like Morse code, and my mind went back to the movie we saw the other night. The one we had our little disagreement about. You can't help how your mind connects things up, can you? So just now I was thinking how that one woman character—I can't remember her name—said that her heart felt like it was shouting 'Mayday! Mayday!'"

"I went to a psychiatrist once, Helen, and she called that a panic attack."

"That's not it exactly—what I'm feeling. But it has qualities of it, I suppose. I think I might have just about had enough of this bleak landscape, beautiful as it is. You know what a French phrase for melancholy is?"

"What?"

"Something like 'black butterflies.' A dark—*fluttering*. Interesting phrase, I think."

I did not know how to follow up on this so I said, "This is a nice little walking tour, isn't it?"

"I'm enjoying it," she said.

Just past the railroad tracks we reached the first of the Granary Ponds, which had ice along its margins. The Granary Ponds comprised a sequence of shallow pools with muddy borders and erratic placement and configurations of boulders, and are a fine place in season to see arctic terns, Bonaparte's gulls, and—in early June—Sabine's gulls. During migration season the ponds are absolutely a cacophony, a cornucopia of birds—ducks, for instance: northern pintail, green-winged teal, American wigeon, northern shoveler, greater scaup, old-squaw, mallard, black duck, gadwall, blue-winged teal, lesser scaup.

However, this was October and turning out to be a day of darkening clouds and temperature drop and on occasion gusting snow, when it had begun with sharp sunlight glinting off the water.

"I've done my homework," Helen said, "and I bet you haven't."

"How so?"

"Can you name the local shorebirds—even though we aren't going to see them for the most part?"

"I can name a few."

Helen closed her eyes and recited, "semipalmated plover, Hudsonian godwit, yellowlegs—no, that would be lesser yellowlegs, ruddy turnstone, red-necked phalarope, snipe, short-billed dowitcher—"

"I get the hint, Helen."

"—dunlin, semipalmated and least and stilt sandpipers. Those are the most common."

"Is it your experience that bird-watchers can be the most competitive people on earth?"

"I'm not competitive," Helen said. "With you, for instance, how challenging might that be? No, I'm just saying the names out loud for enjoyment's sake."

"Guess what? You forgot the buff-breasted sandpiper."

"That is really what you would call 'uncommon' up here. I was naming *common* shorebirds."

At the end of the first Granary pond, we turned left and followed a road back up to the railroad tracks leading out to the docks. The river was moving rapidly here, great, shifting eddies. "I've been here in summer, you know," Helen said.

"You mentioned that. I'd like to come back some summer, too. Maybe next summer."

Helen winced at my obtuse reference to the future, then, generously, somewhat made light of it. "Well, try to find me in the afterlife and give me a report."

"What's French for 'Sorry I said that'?"

"Anyway, as for birds, the summer here is quite remarkable."

"I have a feeling you won't have to refer to your notebooks."

"Parasitic jaegers, arctic loons . . ."

We started to laugh, and Helen said, "And I once saw a Ross's gull out here."

"Maybe a once-in-a-lifetime thing, for most birdwatchers, I bet."

"Well, I have this *goddamn* disease! So it might have to be."

"Have you been in a lot of pain lately?"

"I've just been thinking—"

Helen stared at the river through binoculars and now preferred to talk while studying the river.

"Thinking about what?" I said.

"Thinking about . . . you know, what comes *next*. Is there anything *next*. Which I do not believe in, exactly. Reincarnation. But I have begun to think about it quite a

bit. To see if I might find it useful to believe in. You know—
what is the right word? *Engaging*. Could I locate myself in
the whole concept of it."

"Nothing to lose by thinking about it."

"Don't worry, it's not all black butterflies. It's just—what's
the phrase you Americans use all the time? Trying to 'get my
mind around it.'"

"You look tired. Let's go back. It's getting cold, let's go
back."

Helen kept looking through the binoculars.

"In a minute," she said.

The wind whipped in from the river; I regretted that we
hadn't worn scarves. "See anything out there?" I said.

"A duck of some sort, I think. Stayed late, stayed late."

Five or so minutes of silence; I looked back to see
George smoking a cigarette as he leaned against the truck.
His rifle was racked against the rear window.

"Birds—*a* bird," Helen said, "strikes me as an option. Becoming a bird seems a good choice, don't you think?"

"I don't have much understanding of it, Helen. But I'm
not sure reincarnation is a matter of *choice*."

"I've studied up on this. I'll study up a great deal more.
But so far, I like Buddhist notions of predestination—I like
that a lot. But, still, I can't accept traditional systems of belief. In reincarnation, I mean. You won't know anyway, will
you, if you were right? Because if you become a cow or
a tree, you won't have human memory. So—this is my
point—why not choose? Choose what you'd most prefer to
become."

"Well, I have a lot of days as a human being I'd like to

forget," I said. "And I mean, now, while I'm still here on earth!"

"That's quite funny, I think," Helen said.

There was a sudden ferocious gusting of wind and in unison, like some kind of evolutionary survival tactic, ten or eleven ravens about twenty meters downriver each bent slightly forward, almost as if nailing their beaks into the hard ground, an impressive balletic display of synchronicity. They held that position for a good two minutes, then flapped and squawked off every which way.

"What a weird dream I had last night," Helen said.

"Tell me walking back to the truck."

"It was from a God's-eye view—or, maybe, a bird's-eye view. And all it consisted of was my damn typewriter on the ground. In the snow. And that was it. And then I woke up."

"Maybe you'd already—"

"—become a bird. I know. I've thought of that. But I'm not good at interpreting dreams, you know. I can't somehow place trust in it. That's just me. But I'd allow for that interpretation, sure, why not?"

"No sense of which bird, though."

"I think I've decided."

"Decided which bird you were in the dream, or decided which bird you'd like to become?"

We got to the truck. George climbed into the truck and started the engine and waited. "I've decided to become a bird of . . . the sea . . . and cliffs."

Helen slid in next to George. "You know," I said, "I think I'm going to walk back."

"Want the rifle?" George said.

"No thanks."

"Well you'll be okay—no worry," George said. "But go on, take the rifle. Leave it out front your door at the motel, eh?"

I took the rifle in hand. "See you at supper," I said to Helen.

"At least take the binoculars," Helen said, handing them to me. "See what you can see."

No rhyme or reason to it, but along the railroad tracks I took a single potshot at a lone raven; it was a halfhearted shot, I missed widely, the raven scattered off as if riding on the echo. Out over the river.

How was it possible to even imagine I would ever meet someone for whom *A Field Guide to the Birds* (Peterson, Golden, others) of this or that part of the world, would provide a bevy of possibilities for reincarnation? Yet that is precisely how Helen began to use her field guides. She may have been doing this for some time before we met, I never found out. Paging through the guides, taking notes, circling certain illustrations, underlining behavioral descriptions, moving her finger along passages and data, "my future as a bird at my very fingertips," she wryly stated.

"How are you ever going to narrow down your possibilities?" I asked, perhaps two or three weeks after the subject of reincarnation had been broached.

"I already have," she said. "Look. Let's get something straight, as Americans like to say. Reincarnation's not a desperate way of thinking. My brain's not gone all haywire. Kawabata, I think it was, or some other Japanese writer who killed himself, called suicide 'a bold act of imagination.' I don't agree with that necessarily. That's not what I'm considering anyway, am I? No, I'm not. I'm going to stay alive until I die, and not by my own hand, so let's get that straight. But maybe reincarnation's a bold act of imagination, too. If you want it to be. My mother thought that when you die your soul—which she couldn't describe, and I asked her a hundred times what it looked like when I was a child—went up to heaven. I asked her what heaven looked like, too. She couldn't say.

"At least if I choose a place, a geography—and I have, by the way. If I choose a geography, then at least I can answer the question of what the so-called afterlife's going to look like, can't I?"

"I suppose so," I said.

"There's no 'suppose' to it."

I felt in her room at that moment that if I did not credit her researches and thinking on this matter, I would be banished; there was definitely an unprecedented tension; I felt lacking in the proper resources to debate or dismiss anything. The impassioned plea to comprehend a self-generated theory of reincarnation, then subscribe wholly to it, was not being made to me by Helen (no need for that), but by Helen to herself. To witness this was disquieting.

I was tiptoeing, but moved forward. "So, Helen, what choices have you narrowed it down to, if I may ask? Not one of those ugly shearwaters, or puffins, I hope."

"See, right there! See how you're judging in advance from a human perspective?"

"What other perspective can I judge from?"

"*You* can't find shearwaters particularly attractive, or maybe not interesting, so you think being one would make for a terrible life."

"Okay, I understand. Let's move on. I'm sorry I said that. In fact, I take back everything I've ever said."

"Probably a good idea, but impossible."

"Okay, I know it's a bird that lives by the sea, and maybe nests up in cliffs."

"I said as much, didn't I? Just now my choices are too personal. No offense, Howard Norman. You just need time to think about all of this. You may never understand it, who knows? I have got it down to two or three—and I can say, they all live in my very favorite place I've studied birds."

"Where's that? You've never told me."

"Newfoundland—the Canadian Maritimes. Canada on the Atlantic Ocean—"

"Thanks for telling me that much. It means a lot to me."

"Whether it does or not—"

"Me? If I was going to choose for myself, I'd become a kingfisher."

"I appreciate that you've given it some thought."

"I don't have a set opinion about reincarnation, all I'm saying is, if I could become something it'd be a kingfisher."

"You like that bird far more than I do, in this life, I mean," Helen said, chuckling at her own aesthetic judgment. "Kingfishers seem—what's the phrase? Nuts in the head."

"Don't let looks deceive you."

This made Helen laugh. "I'll let whatever I want deceive me, thank you very much."

―――――

One thing I learned early on was that when Helen dropped by my motel room and said, "Let's talk about—" introducing a subject, it meant she'd already pondered it for quite some time. "Obsessing is a kind of sustenance," she said, which I didn't understand at first, but came to realize, meant, in part, that "obsessing" about something by definition replaced obsessing about cancer. Reincarnation served that purpose.

In my own journal I had registered snippets and summaries, and the whole of conversations I'd had with Helen about reincarnation on the following dates: October 8, October 11, October 12, October 17, October 19, October 23, October 24, October 26, October 29, October 30, and November 1, which is the day we took the train to Winnipeg.

Yet specifically I recall the evening of October 29. Helen sat on my bed, unfolded a map of Canada, and pointed to an area she had circled. "Right there," she said. I turned off my fairly useless transistor radio. She had sectioned off part of Newfoundland. "I've marked the spot where I want my ashes scattered."

"Helen, come on, let's just go to your room and listen to the shortwave or something, all right?"

"You should be happy for me, Howard Norman. I've come to a final decision."

"Newfoundland, okay, but what kind of bird?"

"Cape Freels. I was there twice. The seabirds are . . . plentiful."

"Your medications are making you hallucinate again, I see."

"Ha-ha, very funny. I am quite capable of laughing at myself, but not at this moment."

"Okay, I see where you've marked. Cape Freels. And—?"

"I'm keeping which bird to myself. Please understand."

"Of course. Of course I do."

Helen began to sob, a kind of wracking sob borne up from deep in her chest; she pressed her forehead against the window overlooking the river. "I feel *exactly* how Akutagawa said it, 'a most unhappy happiness.'"

"Happy that you've come to a decision; unhappy you've had to?"

"That's too simple, but honestly, I'd like to not talk about it."

"Let's go over and listen to the shortwave."

"All right." She started out the door without turning to look at me. "How many actual real decisions do we make, in a life? I mean, we all the time say 'yes' or 'no' to all sorts of things, naturally. But Life and Death things, how many? How many?"

GOOD-BYE, GOOD-BYE

On their way to seal-hunting grounds, some hunters saw a big wooden boat stuck in the ice. They took dogsleds over to it. One hunter threw his spear into the boat. The spear stuck in a plank of wood. "Let's pull out this plank and see if it's good for a fire," he said.

"Go away! Get out! Go away!"—they heard a voice call down.

They looked up and saw a man standing on the deck of the boat. He was standing there with three other people.

"Hey—hey! Your boat is stuck in ice!" a hunter said. "You'll be here all winter now!"

"Get us out," this man said.

"Nobody can get this boat loose," the hunter said. "What is your name?"

"Noah."

"Who are the others?"

"My wife, my daughter, my son."

"What's this boat called?"

"An ark."

"On our way back from hunting seals, we'll stop by again. Then you and your family can come back to our village and spend the winter. Just give us a few planks of wood to start a fire with."

"No," said Noah. Just then a big animal walked into view on the ark. It had a large head and curved tusks—it was shivering in the cold.

"It's a woolly mammoth," a hunter said, "except it's not shaggy-haired and the tusks are different and it's shivering. Woolly mammoths don't shiver in the cold!"

"What's that big animal?" another hunter said.

"It's an elephant," Noah said.

"We'll throw some spears up to you," a hunter said. "You kill the elephant, we'll cut it up and haul it back to the village. Everyone will have enough to eat. Then you and your family can stay through the winter."

"No," said Noah. "I have to keep all the animals on my boat. Until we get back home."

"Noah," a man said, "you're stuck in the ice. The winter is long."

"*Father, let's go to the village,*" *said the daughter.* "*Husband, let's go to the village,*" *said the wife.* "*Father, let's go to the village,*" *said the son.*

"*No—no—no,*" *said Noah.*

"*Good-bye, good-bye, good-bye, good-bye,*" *said the hunters. They set out across the ice. But soon a raven landed near them.* "*Turn around—look,*" *said the raven. The raven flew off.*

The hunters turned around. They saw Noah's wife, son, and daughter just behind. "*They've got the wrong clothes,*" *said a hunter.* "*They're already shivering.*"

The hunters let Noah's family catch up and then gave them warm clothes. Now they traveled with the hunters. They were out on the ice for many days, and during this time holes were chiseled through the ice, seals were caught, and many fish were caught. "*How do you like living with us?*" *a hunter asked.*

"*It's good,*" *said Noah's wife.* "*It's good,*" *said the daughter.* "*It's good,*" *said the son.*

The hunters tied seals to their sleds, they got the dogs running well, and everyone went back to the ark. They stood next to it. One hunter shouted up, "*Hey—Noah—look! Look! Here's your family! They enjoy living with us! Come to our village, you can spend the winter. Just pry off a few planks of wood and throw them down. Push a few animals down, too. That's all we ask—some planks, some animals on the ice.*"

"*Come back up,*" *Noah said to his family.*

"*No—good-bye,*" *said Noah's wife.*

Noah then threw down some handfuls of animal shit. It landed on the ice. It steamed there. The hunters looked at it. They had not seen such shapes before, not quite. One hunter said to Noah's wife, "*Tell us how the animals on the ark taste.*"

"*We don't eat them,*" she said.

"*You travel with them. You live on a boat with them. But you don't eat them.*"

"*That's right,*" she said.

"*Well,*" a hunter said, "*we're getting these seals back to our village.*"

"*Father, pry off a few planks of wood and come back with us,*" Noah's son said. With this, Noah flung down some hunks of animal shit. They steamed on the ice.

The hunters and Noah's family set out. When they got to the village, a big meal was prepared. Everyone ate seal and fish. Now Noah's family was living there.

"*How do you like living here?*" an old woman asked Noah's daughter.

"*It's a good thing,*" she said.

"*All right,*" the old woman said, "*why don't you get married. I have someone for you.*"

"*All right,*" Noah's daughter said. She was introduced to a young man and they got married. "*How about my brother?*" Noah's daughter asked.

"*All right,*" the old woman said. Noah's son was introduced to a young woman and they got married. "*How about my mother?*" Noah's son asked.

"*Do you think Noah will leave the ark?*" the old woman said.

"*No,*" he said.

With this, the old woman introduced Noah's wife to a good hunter and they got married. Every few days, Noah's son and daughter left food scraps out near the ark. They looked out from the village. Ravens landed near the food. When the ravens scattered off, they knew that Noah got the food. They said, "*He's not starving.*"

One day a raven landed in the village. It said to Noah's wife, son, and daughter, "Many animals left the ark. They wandered out across the ice. They're gone."

The next day the raven said, "Many colorful birds flew out from the ark out into the distance. They're gone."

The next day the raven said, "More animals are gone."

The next day, Noah's daughter said to the raven, "Tell my father that I got married. Say that my brother got married, too. Say that my mother married a good hunter in this village." The raven flew off with this news.

When the raven landed in the village again, Noah's daughter said, "What did my father say?"

"Good-bye," the raven said. "Good-bye. Good-bye."

Winter was long and there were many days nobody had food to eat. Then there would be luck in hunting and fishing. At such times food scraps were left near the ark. Finally, there came the ice-break-up. The ark was set free-floating again. Noah's son and his wife, Noah's daughter and her husband, paddled out to the ark in kayaks. "Father, look—!" said the daughter—"look at my husband. Look at your son's wife. Look at us!"

Noah sent down a raven. The raven said, "Good-bye."

Noah's daughter and her husband, and Noah's son and his wife paddled back to the village.

One day, a boy ran into the village shouting, "Hey—hey—hey—look!" Everyone went to look. They saw that the ark was low in the water. Then the ark sank. Soon Noah floated in, holding on to some ark planks. When he washed up to shore, a few children grabbed the planks and ran off. Noah came into the village. The children set the planks on a drying rack.

"This is my wife," Noah's son said. "This is my husband,"

Noah's daughter said. "This is now my husband," Noah's wife said. "He's a good hunter."

"Push me along in the southerly direction," Noah said.

So some villagers did as Noah asked. They pushed him along. They gave him some food, too. They watched as Noah walked away. Other villagers paddled out onto the water to collect planks. They got quite a few.

Part IV

THE AFTERLIFE

WRITE ME A LETTER

From my journal, November 8, 1977:

In the Halifax train station Helen wore blue jeans, a white blouse, a gray button-down sweater, white socks, black high-topped tennis shoes she had purchased this morning on Water Street. Helen is taking an evening train to Montreal and then will fly the next day to Amsterdam, London, then on to Tokyo; from there she'll travel to Kyoto to stay with her brother and sister-in-law.

Helen had gotten a haircut, taken a long bath in her room at the Lord Nelson Hotel, bought a few magazines for the train, had a bacon, lettuce, tomato sandwich for lunch at the hotel. I joined her and we talked and drank tea until around four-thirty, when we took a taxi to the train station. She had one suitcase, her trunk, her satchel full of notebooks, ledgers, diaries, and letters. I was to pack up and send her typewriter as soon as possible to Japan. She looked quite pale; sitting on one of the long polished wooden pews in the station, she noticed me noticing and pinched her cheeks. "Coquette," she said.

"A word that hardly applies to you, Helen."

"This is the last time we'll see each other. So, Howard Norman, good-bye. You don't have to wait. I don't mind sitting here alone."

"I mind not spending more time with you, though."

"Fine."

"Good, let's just sit here, then."

"Let's write letters. Write me a letter, I'll write you back."

"Sounds good."

"I need to be more precise about it, I think. How about a letter per week—no, that sounds too often, no matter what. How about a letter every two weeks? You have my brother's address, unless you've lost it?"

"I have it written down."

"Why not let's choose the same two days each month to post a letter?"

"Fine."

"The first and the twentieth."

"Any reason for those?"

"It seems right. To me, they seem right."

"Want to get something to drink?"

"No thank you. I'm not in the least bit thirsty."

"Your train doesn't leave for over an hour. You've got your ticket. Let's just talk."

"I want you to understand that I disapprove in advance, should you fail to send your twice-monthly letters. I've got the one big disappointment, of course. I don't want to suffer small ones, too."

"I can understand that, sure."

"The train's in-station, you know. I could board early. You could take in a movie."

"If you want, Helen, I'll take the train with you to Montreal."

"Completely uncalled for."

"I haven't been on a train in a year or so."

"I'm going to sit and read my books. I'm going to work on my notes. I've always found trains good to work on, you see. Unless, of course, one has the bad fortune of being seated next to a snotty, crying child whose parents don't care that—"

"What? That you're translating a story from Inuit into Japanese—a story about Noah's Ark! Imagine saying *that* to someone on a train. Someone who says, 'What are you working on, there, if I may ask?'"

"Life can be quite odd, can't it?"

"You know what I noticed? I noticed that one thing you really loved—it always cracked you up—was the kinds of temper tantrums Noah had. In Mark's stories. You know, how he'd come all unhinged."

"Come all unhinged—that's nice. I'm going to write that down."

"Suit yourself."

"No, you're right, I do love those moments. Noah unhinged."

"I doubt the train's going to be very crowded."

"I think you're right."

"Helen, we're not talking out loud about what we're really thinking, are we? Or am I wrong about that?"

"This thing. My 'condition,' you mean—well why talk about it, here and now? I will say this. Illness tends to turn you inward; it makes you eccentric in ways you never wanted. It's hard to explain."

"Will you see your doctors in Japan again?"

"Of course—but the news won't change. I've had diagnoses in America, England, and Japan. Same news, same news, same news."

"You'll be with your family. That's good."

"Stop trying so goddamn hard. It's getting on my nerves."

"I think I'm taking the train to Montreal."

"You, Howard Norman, are not invited."

"Can you sleep on airplanes, Helen?"

"On a long flight, yes."

"Not me. I'd be awake staring at the seat in front of me. I'm a bad flier. I don't have a good time."

"Too bad. That's really a shame."

"Still, you know what? I'd go—I'd fly to Japan, you know, just to see where you live."

"Write me a letter over there. We'll see what happens. The thing about flying is, you have to look down and think of painters like Cézanne. High over farmland, think of Cézanne and then you see things nicely. Then you're glad for the view."

"I'd have to study up on Cézanne's paintings first."

"Yes, go in that order."

"Maybe later I'll fly to Japan."

"I wouldn't be able to give you the Grand Tour, you know. I'd be able to give you some advice on where to travel in the country, though."

"I guess we start with letters."

"If you feel like walking around outside, go ahead. I'll wait here."

"No, I'm fine."

"Can you see if they sell tea?"

I bought a cup of tea and delivered it to Helen in a paper cup. Arrivals and departures were clicking in on the overhead panel. Montreal was now fourth down. The first three were local, that is, had destinations within Nova Scotia. When I next looked at Helen I saw that she had fallen asleep, the cup of tea still clutched in her hands, though precariously tilted. I managed without waking her to slip the cup from her hands and set it on the bench.

Over the next five or so minutes Helen leaned left in her sleep until finally she was lying down sideways; I woke her ten minutes before her train was called for boarding.

"Why'd you let me sleep?" she said, quite annoyed.

"I just watched it happen. You looked peaceful."

"Dumb excuse, if you think about it."

"Come on, it's Gate Two."

"Wait, I've got something for you." She opened her satchel and took out a manila envelope and handed it to me. "Please don't open this until— Let's be direct, all right. My brother, Artie, will let you know when. He'll telephone you."

"Helen—"

"*In Fond Remembrance of Me*—that's what I've titled my little missive."

"For safekeeping, that's for sure. Maybe I should buy an actual safe for it."

"A desk drawer will suffice."

"All right, then. It's Gate Two."

We did not speak on our way down the stairs. Her trunk had been brought on directly from the luggage room, but I carried her suitcase onto the train. Helen looked around and found a seat about halfway on the left side. I slid her suitcase onto the overhead rack. She put her satchel on the seat. There were only two other people in Helen's car, an elderly woman and a teenage boy. I could hear the low staticky buzz of his transistor radio. Then Helen changed her mind and said, "Would you carry my bag up front a little way?" She moved to near the front of the car. Now she seemed pleased. She set out her notebooks and magazines. We held hands, in the manner of two children about to skip rope, I mean, and almost immediately let go. She nodded sharply and sat down, but I stayed standing near her seat and looked out the window.

A conductor stepped into the car at the far end and said, "Tickets." Helen turned to the window; possibly she saw my reflection in the glass, possibly not. "Don't forget me," she said.

BAD TEMPER

In church I heard about Noah's Ark. In the place it was built there were bad people. God caused a flood, and Noah—this man named Noah—was sent floating away on the boat with his family. They traveled around, and what happened was, they got lost.

They drifted into Hudson Bay, is what happened. They arrived at the beginning of winter, is what happened. And—oh, oh, oh— this Noah had a very bad temper. One day, just when the ark was caught in the ice for the rest of the winter, some villagers went out to talk to Noah. They found out his name and found out that the big wooden boat was called "ark." "Come on, come on," a man said to this Noah, "come on, come to our village with your family."

"No, you'll kill us," Noah said.

"Why?"

"To get the animals I have on my ark," Noah said.

"If you give us some, we won't have to kill you to get them."

"Let's go into the village," Noah's wife said.

"No," said Noah.

"We work hard to get animals to eat—we could go out on the ice—hunting is dangerous—we get out there—we fall through the ice—and here you only have to turn around and there's big animals to eat—why don't you?"

"My family eats other things—we don't eat these animals," Noah said.

"That is stupid—oh, hey, what about if we help you? We'll show you how to hunt seals. We'll show you how to fish through the ice."

"No, we'll stay on the ark," said Noah.

Villagers gave Noah's wife, son, and daughter some winter bundling. In their bundling, they went with the villagers out on the ice. Noah wasn't happy about this. He got into a bad temper. He fell to the deck, wailed, and spit—a bad temper.

Out on the ice, Noah's wife, son, and daughter were taught. They caught some seals. They pulled in some fish. They cleaned them. Seeing this, Noah ran out on the ice. He crammed his hand down a breathing-hole and a seal bit him—it bit his thumb.

"Look at those teeth marks on your thumb," a man said. "Noah, you have angered the seals. Now they'll go away. Let's go to another place to hunt them."

Noah went back to the ark. His family went with the villagers.

They were gone many days. When they got back, Noah's son said, "Good hunters taught us well. We caught many seals and fish."

"Look at both your thumbs," Noah's wife said.

"Yes, while you were away out on the ice, I stuck my hands in breathing-holes. Seals bit them."

"Your husband is the only one we've ever known to show his bad temper in this manner," a man said. "Look at his thumbs— look at them!"

With that, Noah's thumbs fell off. They were plucked up by gulls. Noah fell to the deck of the ark. He wept. He spit. His family stayed, then, on the ark—all the rest of the winter. Noah was instructed not to cram hands into seal breathing-holes—he tried a few times when he got angry, but his family caught him at it and dragged him back to the ark. They looked at his hands for teeth marks of seals.

This happened a long time ago, but it happened as I tell it. When the ice-break-up arrived, Noah and his family floated away on the ark. But ice had cracked the bottom of the ark. The ark leaked in water and it sank. Some village men paddled kayaks out—the ark was gone and they couldn't find Noah, Noah's wife, Noah's son, or Noah's daughter.

"Maybe they reached shore somehow," a man said. "Maybe they reached a village to the south, somehow," another said. "Maybe they are drying their clothes out somewhere," another said. "Maybe," another said.

THE SEA AND CLIFFS

In early August 1978, a few weeks before I returned to Churchill, Manitoba, I stood on a cliff near Cape Freels, Newfoundland, and scattered Helen Tanizaki's ashes to the wind. There were a lot of seabirds around. Cape Freels is located between Newton and Lumsden, reached by tributary road off the Trans-Canada Highway. A decade earlier Helen had watched seabirds from pretty much this same spot, according to a letter she sent from Kyoto. She and her Dutch husband, Cees, had spent "a relatively calm," as she had put it, final week of their turbulent marriage visiting outports in Nova Scotia and Newfoundland. Having flown to Halifax from London, they drove to Trinity Bay, where they spent the night in a village called—ironically, considering the dilapidated state of their marriage—Salvage. The next morning they drove to Cape Freels.

In Cape Freels they spent two days walking and birdwatching. "And nothing much else to speak of," Helen wrote. They had intended an additional day of hiking but instead decided to turn back. "I look back on it as the saddest of belated honeymoons possible. Still, we were friends."

From Helen's letters and our conversations in Churchill and Halifax, I gathered that Helen and Cees suspected that they had been far too impetuous in getting married and felt they had aged badly within marriage. Helen had married Cees, an architecture student in Paris, when she was studying mythology and linguistics at the Collège de France. The marriage lasted not quite two years. "Cees was a nice man," Helen had said, "but too fearful." Ending the farewell honeymoon, they returned by ferry to Halifax, stayed near Historic Properties, and a few days later Cees left for San Francisco, where he joined an architectural firm. In order to finish her doctorate in linguistics Helen returned to Inuit communities in Greenland, Baker Lake, and other locales throughout the arctic. "Now and then," she said, "Cees and I exchanged letters. Basically we got divorced through the mail. The letters were very formal. Then they stopped altogether, by mutual agreement, I suppose, but never declared."

Helen's mother was British, her father Japanese—Clare and Seicho. Clare was a school nurse, Seicho an engineer specializing in bridges; they had met when seated by happenstance next to each other's table in a Kyoto teahouse. Clare had traveled with two other women on holiday to Japan; the other two women had stayed behind in Tokyo while Clare visited Kyoto. Helen was in fact born in London but raised from ages three to fifteen in Kyoto. She had a brother two years younger named Arthur, whom Helen called Artie-san. A week before her sixteenth birthday her family returned to Europe, where they had houses in London and Scotland. (Her father preferred Scotland.) "We took a family trip once to the Hebrides," she said. By age eighteen Helen was fluent in Japanese, English, and French. "I was drawn to languages." Arthur met and married Susanne and settled in Kyoto, where he completed a three-year apprenticeship in bookbinding and set up his own business, which included the buying and selling of rare editions. Susanne eventually became Helen's closest friend. Susanne and Arthur had two daughters, both of whom were receiving a British education, in boarding schools.

In legal papers Helen had instructed Arthur, whom I had never met, to allow me to disperse her ashes specifically "off the Newfoundland coast at Cape Freels." By telephone I suggested to Arthur that Helen's ashes be sent to the central post office in St. Johns, Newfoundland, and I would retrieve them there. I was in Toronto at the time and said that I would immediately leave for St. Johns. Arthur and I spoke for ten or so minutes, that is all. Within the first moment of conversation, however, I could tell he wished to settle things quickly. That is, he got directly to the point. I intervened with condolences. He replied with a curt "Thanks very much," spoken with an accent that so resembled Helen's it caused me a veritable déjà vu. Anyway, my suggestion about where to send Helen's ashes was accepted as logical and expedient, given, as Arthur put it, "the narrow consideration of my sister's request." I said, "Okay, then, Arthur. Thank you for calling me." He rang off.

I knew from Helen's letters that she had certainly mentioned to Arthur a number of things about our friendship, what things, however, I'll never know. In my own letters I kept Helen apprised of my whereabouts. The long and short of it, though, was that I was not tied to any schedule; it was easy for me to set right out for St. Johns. Besides, what could possibly be a more pressing commitment? Still, when

I hung up the phone I wondered if Arthur perhaps wasn't bewildered, even angered, by Helen's posthumous assignation with me and Cape Freels—I wondered, too, what if anything she had shared with her brother about her imagining of the afterlife. Perhaps Arthur had preferred for Helen to remain in Japan.

In St. Johns I rented a car at the airport and drove to the post office. I signed all the customs forms and was handed a small package. Then I drove to Cape Freels.

The wind that day was truly wild. It literally whistled in one's ears. The sea air was ventriloquial: the keening of gulls seemed to ricochet off an invisible wall far to my left, whereas the actual gulls were sailing off to my right. Sailing and keening and crying and wheeling. In what seemed no more than a mile offshore, I viewed through binoculars Cory's shearwaters eddying in great numbers around an iceberg. Icebergs in August were not all that uncommon a sight in these waters. Every so often as I stood there a gust of cold wind seemed to sweep in directly from the berg, which looked capable of producing its own weather system. On the flight up from Halifax our pilot had in fact circled above this iceberg on behalf of tourists on board, taking us "just a little bit out of our way." From the air it looked like a white planet floating in blue-black space. Now, standing atop a cliff, I could distinguish the darker blue of the current, but such was the iceberg's enormous illusion of fixity that I had to study it through binoculars to determine that it was actually drifting. Waves lapped up against it.

In its transport south to Canadian waters, wind had

eroded, gouged, and hollowed the iceberg; near the center
of its upper tier were three vaguely human shapes; it all resembled a Henry Moore sculpture of an amorphous parent
sitting with two amorphous children. Shearwaters, perhaps
having hitched a ride for days, swirled from their shoulders.

Through binoculars I noticed, too, puffins, the comical
pudgy, gaudy-billed birds, excellent divers which old-time
fishermen called "parrots of the sea." However, the puffins
mostly kept to the opposite side of the iceberg, now and
then catapulting up into view, looping crazily, then dropping
below the horizon of ice again. I looked at the puffins
awhile. I thought about Helen: *Which bird—what type of bird
are you?* Then I was aware of someone and turned to find
an old scruffy-bearded fellow standing next to his battered
pickup about twenty meters from where I stood. He was
casting me a hard stare and had left his truck door open.
He was lanky, slightly stooped, and wore a double layer of
sweaters, black rough trousers, fisherman's galoshes, one
buckled up to the top while the other flapped open. Both of
his thumbs were bandaged. Finally he sidled up beside me,
nodded hello, leaned over the cliff, and in a thick Scottish
accent said, "Dizzy down sheer." Without another word he
walked back to his truck, climbed in, and drove off. Yet he
had struck a useful note of caution; indeed it was a harrow-
ingly steep line of vision between the overhang and the sea
where, in between floating woven rugs of slick kelp, I occasionally glimpsed a shadowy whale.

After an hour or so of mindlessly gazing at seabirds, I remembered a letter in which Helen wrote, "The Ainu people

of Hokkaido in northern Japan are capable of what they call 'travel off the earth,' or something like that. They have shamans who stare at birds until their minds fly out of their bodies. Enviable talent, don't you agree?"

Of course I did agree, and right then and there at Cape Freels I wanted to attempt it, just somehow to show Helen that I wasn't afraid of the experience. To fly out of myself. But the sad truth was, my new hiking boots were hurting and blistering my feet; I was stuck in the quotidian world, the earthly domain.

Not so Helen, though. I unwrapped the brown paper. Tucked inside the cloth wrapping was a small envelope. I slid out its note. In her elegant English cursive Helen had written: "As long as you are there, you may as well look at birds. Try for a moment to set me apart from the others." I opened the beautiful black lacquer box on which was depicted a flight of three Japanese cranes, then held it at arm's length above my head. Crosswinds scooped out the ashes, casting them like charcoal confetti every which way, and some even flew back into my face and across my shoulders. Gulls came by for a look; nothing they could use, nothing, for that matter, they probably could even catch.

Quite an unusual moment, I felt, delivering Helen's ashes to the place she had foreseen as the plausible afterlife for her, should it work out that she became a bird of the sea and cliffs. It was gratifying, surprisingly not sad. In my life I have regretted nothing less. What could be more of a gift than to follow dear Helen's instructions, to follow through on what, in a letter, she referred to as "my attempt at reincarnation." I

myself did not believe in it, not just then, at least, but was
privileged to convey Helen into her belief. Once all the
ashes had disappeared, once I had brushed ashes from my
face and jacket and boots, I read Helen's note again and then
did something I had never done before or have done since,
laughed until I cried.

YES AND NO

*When a wooden boat floated into Hudson Bay, villagers went out
in kayaks to it. When they got there, they heard coughing-choking
noises. Then they heard "Yes—yes—yes" choked out of a man's
throat, and saw a man stumble to the railing of the big wooden boat.*

*This man choked out "Yes" again, and suddenly gull feathers
flew from his mouth and he spoke clearly, "Go away!"*

"What is your name?" a villager asked.

"My name is Noah."

"What's your boat called—what kind of boat is this?"

"An ark."

*"Why were you choking, why were you choking and saying
'Yes'?"*

"A man made white bird feathers fly down my throat."

"Why did he do that?"

*"He wanted planks of wood from my ark for a fire. He wanted
the big animals below deck. He wanted to marry my wife."*

"Where is your family?"

*With this, Noah's wife, son, and daughter stepped into view.
"Here they are," this Noah said.*

"*What sorts of animals are below deck?*" *a village man asked.*

"*Many kinds,*" *Noah's wife said.*

"*It's the shaman—a very powerful man—who made feathers fly down your throat. He's around here now. He stays for as long as he wants,*" *the village man said.*

"*That man took planks of wood and a few animals,*" *said Noah's daughter.*

"*Yes,*" *said another man,* "*when his fire has gone out—when he has eaten all the animals he took—he'll come back.*"

"*Will he go after my wife?*" *said Noah.*

"*Yes,*" *a man said.*

"*Better bring your family to our village,*" *a man said.* "*The shaman won't trouble you there. But he'll take all the planks— he'll eat all the animals.*"

"*No—I'll stay here,*" *said this Noah.*

"*Winter is here soon,*" *a man said.* "*That means snow. That means ice. That means bitter cold.*"

The villagers returned home and winter arrived. The ark got stuck in the ice. The shaman came by once—he came by again— he came by again—he stole planks. He stole animals. He choked this Noah with gull feathers—he choked this Noah with colorful bird feathers from the ark. Each time Noah choked, he choked out "*Yes—yes—yes*" *the shaman then had permission to take planks, to take animals. That is how it went. That is what happened.*

One day, when some villagers visited the ark, they saw a few planks fly off the ark out into the distance over the ice. Then they saw two big striped horses tumble out over the ice into the distance. "*What are those animals called?*" *a man said to Noah.*

"*Zebra.*"

"*Zebra—zebra—zebra—zebra,*" *villagers said, trying out the word.*

Out on the ice, the shaman killed the two zebras and made a fire with the planks. He ate some zebra meat.

"*My ark is getting smaller—I'm losing my animals,*" *cried Noah.*

"*Give us a few planks, we'll take you to our village,*" *a man said.*

"*No,*" *said Noah.*

Just then, some village men climbed onto the ark. They went below deck. When they came back up they were choking. They were spitting out colorful bird feathers. When they spit them out, one man said, "There's many strange birds down there—we choked on their feathers."

"*Get back down there, get a few birds!*" *a man said. "Let's see if they taste as good as ptarmigan!*"

"*No—no!*" *the feather-choked men said. They climbed back down onto the ice.*

It went on in such a way for the rest of the winter. Villagers brought food out to the ark for Noah and his family. But the shaman kept choking all of them—Noah, his wife, his son, his daughter— With gull feathers, raven feathers, colorful bird feathers from the ark, the shaman choked them. And each time, Noah said, "Yes—yes—yes." The shaman had a very good winter.

When the ice-break-up began, the ark looked like a big animal with its ribs sticking up—a big dead animal—the ice was breaking apart around Noah and his family. Some villagers paddled out to help. When they got there, Noah's wife said, "Before he left, the shaman choked us."

"*If you come back on another ark, he'll choke you again,*" *a*

man said. Because they did not want to be choked by raven feath-
ers, colorful bird feathers, or gull feathers, Noah and his family did
not come back to Hudson Bay. They paddled kayaks to the south—
a few colorful birds above the kayaks, a few trailing behind—gone
into the horizon. That is my story.

EPILOGUE: THE KIMONO

The following year, 1978, I returned to Churchill, again toward the end of August. It was not without trepidation that I had signed back on to work with Mark Nuqac, this time to translate stories containing a variety of motifs, from shamanism to hunting to vengeance, especially that of the omnipresent goddess-spirit of the arctic sea, Sedna, who is almost continually agitated at the behavior of human beings. (Sedna, of course, now has a planet named after her, the coldest in our solar system.) I was also to work with two other Inuit storytellers at Eskimo Point. Hired by a now-disbanded concern called the Native Canadian Oral History Project out of Winnipeg (at one-quarter the museum's salary), I hoped to transcribe—and at least begin translating—ten of Mark's stories in the month of September. Once again I flew with Driscoll Petchey (who, if anything, was even more talkative; in his three-seater I was a captive audience) to Churchill. Once again I set up in the Beluga Motel, this time in Room 2. I was the motel's only resident. Still, I consciously avoided checking into either Room 1 or Room 10, vigilant, almost superstitious, about how immediate Helen's and my conversations still felt, the CBC pro-

grams we shared, the sound of typing. Rooms may be inter-
changeable, not memories of rooms.

Predictably enough, my work with Mark Nuqac pro-
ceeded in fits and starts. I vowed to take nothing personally,
either in his attitude or behavior toward me. Often, at a potentially incendiary point in our working session, I feigned
composure, offered a patient nod, and smiled till the storm
passed. Noting this, Mark seemed irked. This time he
couldn't "get my goat." (Though he did rouse me once or
twice.) It was pretty much the same old Mark that I had
known a year earlier; the same Mark that Helen saw through
a clearer lens, with more empathy, with far more know-how
in working one-on-one with native speakers, and with the
awareness, I suppose, that Mark was all but mesmerized by
her very presence, which I don't to this day think an exaggeration. Autumn 1978, the few times Mark spoke of
Helen, he did so in a rather cursory manner. But I knew he
harbored deep feelings. "I got a letter from my daughter
Helen," he said. "My wife read it to me."

One good thing, I got to know Mary Nuqac better. She
and Mark were sharing the same house with Mary's young-
est brother, William, and his French-Canadian/Cree wife,
"Josey," short for Josephine, and their three young children.
(The oldest, an eight-year-old boy, slept in the kitchen.)
Mary had become, it seemed, more sullen. She had had another operation in January. She was drinking more. I had
two meals with her—we just ate sandwiches sitting out-
doors—and we had some lengthy conversations; it was by
unspoken agreement that we did not discuss my work with

Mark. She did offer a tidbit of encouragement: "Mark told me you got a little better at hearing how we talk."

And I suppose I had. In December 1977 I had moved back to Ann Arbor, Michigan, where I had recently completed an intermittent residence in the Society of Fellows, affiliated with the University of Michigan. But I kept my one-room apartment in Toronto and frequently stayed there. (In fact, I still hadn't entirely made up my mind if I should become a Canadian citizen since it seemed I was having better luck finding work in that country.) Anyway, Helen had put me in touch with a native Inuit speaker, Michael Smith (he had given up his Inuit name) from Eskimo Point. He was working part-time in a shoe store, part-time in night security at the University of Michigan. Michael Smith was fifty-one, living in a room above a garage on State Street, not far from my own small apartment on Elm Street. I paid him ten dollars an hour for three-hour "language lessons" and was insistent on fitting in as many as our schedules allowed. (I didn't have much of one.) In fact, he was quite organized as a teacher. What's more, he always wore a suit and tie for our lessons, this Inuit man who in February of that year had been named "Employee of the Month" by the shoe store's manager. Though he had forsaken much of his native identity (his fiancée had asked him to convert to Catholicism), he voiced strong opinions about his culture. "I think about where I am from every day. I think about my parents and my brothers and sisters. But I cannot live there." He was—in his own words—"dead set" against the translation work I had done and hoped to continue, as the opportunity afforded itself. When I pressed him on this point, he only said, "So much gets taken." I asserted that Western culture—apparently I felt I could speak on its behalf—"needs the entirely different sensibility of Inuit stories." "Needs them for what?" he said. Just that brief exchange and we were at a tense impasse. We cut the lesson short. From then on we kept exclusively to vocabularies and contexts and exercises he invented, which I found challenging and useful. In late March 1978 Michael Smith dropped by my apartment to say that he had gotten married and was moving to Minneapolis. He gave me a soapstone sculpture depicting a seal disappearing through the ice; just the rear third and tail of the seal was present, the rest of its body had to be imagined. I was surprised at his gift—it might well be considerd "taken" from the Inuit culture, though art cooperatives all over the arctic exported soapstone sculptures.

"Thank you," I said.

"I was going to give you one of a seal just coming up for air."

"Well, this one is fine. Thank you."

"You're welcome."

"No matter what you think, I need this. It'll get me to think about things."

"What things?"

I thought we might be headed into bad weather again. "Sculpture—for one. What else? What it might feel like to dive under the ice."

"Okay, I get it," he said. "Stop before you make a worse fool of yourself."

"Congratulations on your marriage," I said. We shook hands; my language lessons of that sort ended. They had cost me $1,200.

On the morning of September 27, 1978, my last day in Churchill (I would not visit again until the summer of 1981), Mary Nuqac showed me the kimono that Helen had sent from Kyoto. We were standing in the kitchen. She unfolded it from the box it had arrived in and held it up for my appraisal. "It's beautiful," I said. It was white silk, with magnificent embroidered flowers which looked like you could lean over and actually smell their fragrances.

"When did it get here?" I said.

"November."

"Have you tried it on yet?"

"Yes. I wore it one day. Over my sweaters."

Mary folded the kimono again and set it in the box. "Helen wrote a letter to me," Mary said. "She wrote one to my husband. We each got one." Mary looked pensive. "Do you have a picture of Helen?"

"A photograph? We never took any—of each other, I mean. I didn't even have a camera with me."

"I wanted to ask since you got here."

"Helen did send me a photograph from Kyoto. She was in bed." (I didn't mention that, unless I was greatly mistaken, it was a hospital bed.) I touched both of my shoulders. "She had the blanket pulled up to here. Behind her on the wall was a beautiful Japanese scroll."

"A—*scroll?*"

"Yes, it's a tall picture. Probably very old. Someone painted it with special brushes and ink. Black ink. It showed a person beginning a journey. A long walk."

"What else was in the picture?"

"Flying birds."